Monsters, Cryptids, and M

Monsters, Cryptids, and Myst€
And Where to Search for
Maryland and Beyond.

MW01069237

ISBN-13: 978-1-940087-38-2

21 Crows Dusk to Dawn Publishing, 21 Crows, LLC

Always follow the rules/regulations in the areas you seek monsters. Don't trespass. Don't enter areas after dark if it is not allowed.

Monsters/Cryptids

Maryland

Snarly Yow—Black Dog of South Mountain   7

Snallygaster—Terror in the Sky Over South Mountain   12

Dwayyo—Bushy-tailed Dogman   18

Sykesville Monster—Close Encounter with an Ape-Man   22

Goatman—Goatman of Fletchertown Road   25

Chesapeake Bay Chessie—Sea Serpent in Chesapeake Bay   30

West Virginia

Hellhound—Black Dogs in Martinsburg   34

Appalachian Chupacabra—Mysterious Goatsucker of Putnam County   36

Tommyknockers—Tricksters of Brandy Gap Tunnel   38

Flatwoods Monster—Flatwoods-Home of the Green Monster   42

Mothman—Mason County Monster   48

Sheepsquatch—Sheepsquatch of Point Pleasant   59

Flying Ray—Horton Horror—Stingray in the Sky   61

Wampus Cat—Undead Cat of King Shoals   63

White Thing—White Thing of Morgan Ridge   72

Grafton Monster—Riverside Drive Monster   76

Ogua—Monongahela River Two-Headed Turtle   78

Ohio River Monster—Giant Serpent on the Ohio River   80

Cumberland Dragon—Acid-spitting Goosefoot   81

Marrtown Banshee—Marrtown's Foretelling Screamer   83

Monsters/Cryptids

Giant Bird—Spruce Knob's Modern Roc   85

Grant Town Goon—Coal Mine Dump Goon   90

Wendigo—Clicking Flesh-eater   91

Vegetable Man—Bloodsucking Alien   95

The Bigfoot—   97

   Flatwoods/Sutton—Wild Man   100

   Monongahela/Richwood—Ya-hoo   102

   Marlinton —Apple Devil   105

   Blackwater Falls—Canyon Monster   107

   **Canaan Valley National Wildlife   111
   Refuge**—Bigfoot

   New River Gorge—Bigfoot   113

   Webster County—The Hairy One   116

   Monongahela National Forest—Yellow Gape   118

   Polk Gap/Poke Holler—Polk Gap/Poke Holler   120
                              Monster

   Seneca Rocks—Ghillie Beast   126

Ohio

Bigfoot

   Cleveland Metro Parks Rocky River—Bigfoot   129

   Cuyahoga Valley National Park—Bigfoot   131

   Salt Fork State Park—Bigfoot   134

   Hocking Hills Region—Grassman   141

Monsters/Cryptids

Wild Man of Gallipolis—Wild Man or Bigfoot?   144

Minerva Monster—Minerva's Bigfootish Beast   146

Loveland Frogman—Loveland's Legendary Cold-Blooded Cryptid   150

Ohio River Sea Serpent—Cincinnati Serpent   157

Crosswick Monster—An Ohio Dragon   159

Cedar Bog Monster—Peeping Fen Monster   162

Devil Monkey—Iron Furnace Devil Monkey   164

Delphos Dogman—Black Swamp Beasts   166

Defiance Werewolf—A Werewolf in Defiance   168

Charles Mill Lake—Green-Eyed Monster   171

Charles Mill Lake—Orange Eye Sewer Monster   174

Peninsula Python—Travelin' Circus Snake that Got Away and Terrorized a Town   176

Camp Manatoc—Red Eye Madman of Camp Manatoc   183

Melon Heads—Dr. Crowe's Bulbous-Headed Babes   185

South Bay Bessie—Lake Erie's Sea Monster   188

Pennsylvania

Storm Hag of Presque Isle—Lake Erie Storm Hag   193

Kentucky

Goat-Man of Pope Lick Trestle— Pope Lick Monster   199

Citations

204

Mammals, birds, and beasts of any sort fail to see the invisible boundary lines between town or city or state that we humans define. Many of the monsters of Ohio extend into West Virginia. Many of West Virginia cross into Maryland or vice versa.

Since many sites can be visited and to form some pattern (albeit a bit raggedy at times due to the nature of wandering beasts), I've started with the Maryland creatures and worked my way toward West Virginia where many legends have intertwined and then into Ohio and extended it to certain points in Pennsylvania.

The Monsters of Maryland

Monster/Cryptid	Map #
Snarly Yow	1
Snallygaster	2
Dwayyo	3
Sykesville Monster	4
Goatman of Prince George's County	5
Chesapeake Bay Chessie	6

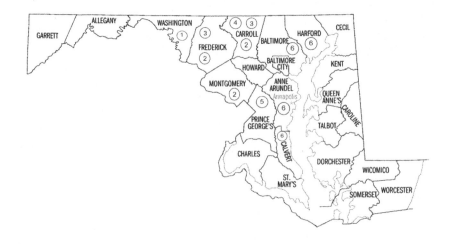

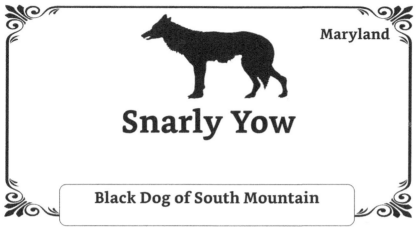

Maryland

Snarly Yow

Black Dog of South Mountain

Description: Huge, tar-black dog. Bushy tail. Solitary. Shadowlike. Grows longer and longer across the road blocking access end to end so travelers cannot pass. Glowing eyes. Fierce red mouth.

Other Names: Black Dog. Werewolf. Dog-Fiend.

Location: Originally found on the west side of South Mountain barring travelers along Old National Pike (Washington County, MD). The range extends, then, from Boonsboro, MD—Washington County to Harpers Ferry, WV —Jefferson County.

Old National Pike where the Snarly Yow would guard the road.

In Maryland, South Mountain stretches southward from the Pennsylvania border to the Potomac River. Along its course are forests and farmland, small towns, and the Appalachian Trail. One of those old byways, the National Pike, forges through at Turner's Gap (a wind gap in the South Mountain Range) near Boonsboro. At the top, a flourishing 21-room tavern/inn was built in the late 1700s by Robert Turner. The property was sold in 1876 to Madeleine Dahlgren, a wealthy widow, and turned into a private residence. Then, in the 1920s, it became a tavern again. Over the years, it became a welcome stopping point for travelers taking the climb to the top—waggoneers, stagecoach drivers, teamsters, and tourists.

It is here along the mountain that the story of the Snarly Yow began. As nightfall would set over the sprinkling of rural cabins and homes on the side of South Mountain, this shadowy dog would slip from wherever its hiding place was in the forest during the daylight. It took the same narrow path until it crossed the dirt road. There, it continued downward until it came to a small and meandering stream where it would disappear.

South Mountain Inn along the Old National Pike where a monstrous shadowy dog, the Snarly Yow, stalks those passing along the roadway. Perhaps you will see this mysterious wolf-like creature when you are driving past—6132 Old National Pike, Boonsboro, MD 21713 (39.484622, -77.620610)

Madeleine Dahlgren's private family chapel atop South Mountain and along the Appalachian Trail—Dahlgren's Chapel—1452 Dahlgren Road, Middletown, MD 21769 (39.484477, -77.618873) The Snarly Yow seemed to have a particular liking of chasing those who had imbibed too freely of liquor and were rowdy traveling past the little church.

If the beast would not have been monstrous in size and had minded its own business, locals would have probably mistaken it for a farmer's wandering dog. But it had a strangeness about it as a thirty-year-old local family man named William would attest in the late 1800s. One evening around ten o'clock, the strapping farmer was returning from the store in Boonsboro. It was a clear night, and the road was easy to see. But just as William reached a particular part of the trail, a huge black dog appeared from the brush and would not allow the man to pass. William pushed forward as if to go around, but the dog grew in length enough to cover the entire road from one side to the other! Its mouth grinned at him, disturbingly wide and bloody red. Undaunted, William rushed at the creature, arm whipping downward to beat it back, but his fists met no resistance and struck the air. The dog bit and clawed back. Again and again, William fought the dog. Then just as quickly as it had appeared, it disappeared. Later, upon holding up his arms, William saw no bruises or cuts. He was utterly unharmed, barring the emotional toll the battle had left with him.

A circuit-riding preacher traveling along the road to one of the local churches ran into the ghostly dog one night. Prudent, the man always rode with rifle ready. When the beast came upon him, he lifted his gun and shot at it with deadly accuracy. He considered himself a sure-shot, never missing his intended target. As the bullets flew, they went right through the dog. Many travelers along the road threw sticks at the Snarly Yow, but their weapons also met no fur or bone. A farmer's wife in a sleigh watched the mysterious black dog disappear and reappear right before her eyes.

Others have come into contact with the Snarly Yow and not just along the National Pike cutting through the South Mountain. It is seen by hikers along the Appalachian Trail on the mountain and even near Harpers Ferry. When approached, it fades away. Recently, a couple traveling along the road in their car hit a giant black dog. After hearing the sound of bone-crushing and the thud of the body underneath, they were able to stop. But when they got out of the car to look, there was no dog beneath. There was only the solitary shadow of a dog on the road behind them snarling.

Where can you look for the Snarly Yow?

Take a hike along the Appalachian Trail—About 17 miles of the trail follows South Mountain into Harpers Ferry. Hikers have seen the creature along the route—

6127 Old National Pike in Boonsboro, MD 21713 (39.484996, -77.619933) to Harpers Ferry, West Virginia 25425 (39.323673, -77.734139).

Weverton Cliff Trail

Weverton Cliffs *(South Mountain) Along the Appalachian Trail, Knoxville, MD 21758 (39.333424, -77.676774)*
Weverton Cliffs Parking Lot*—Weverton Cliffs Road, Knoxville, MD 21758 (39.333157, -77.683358) Tip of South Mountain. Park and head 400 feet southeast on Weverton Cliff Road to Appalachian Trail at the end of the road. Appalachian Trail 704 Weverton Road Knoxville, MD 21758 (39.332781, -77.682179)*

Weverton Cliff View Hike round trip—3 miles. Steep.

Maryland Heights*. Just a few miles drive from Weverton Cliffs. 2.8 mile round-trip.*

Maryland Heights*—hike from Harpers Ferry up the mountain. You might also find a Snarly Yow along the path. Harpers Ferry Road, Knoxville, MD 21758 (39.325322, -77.725596)*

Maryland

Snallygaster

Terror in the Sky Over South Mountain

Description: Part-bird, part-reptile. Later reports suggest metal beak. Razor-sharp teeth. May have octopus tentacles sliding easily from the mouth.

Other Names: Snollygaster.

Location: Central Maryland including Frederick, Montgomery, and Carroll Counties in MD and sweeping into Jefferson County, WV, and even into southern OH

Part-bird and part-reptile, some believe the Snallygaster resembles an extinct Archaeopteryx or Dakota Raptor. It was seen on old roads like this one in Frederick County, MD.

With the settling of the country in the 1730s by German immigrants in Maryland, Pennsylvania, and Virginia, along with these hardy souls, came their customs, folklore, and supernatural beings. One such creature they brought with them is the Snallygaster—the name originating from the German term *Schnelle Geeschter*, which translates to *quick ghosts*—dragon-like ghouls that swooped down from the sky to seize their unwary prey. Back then, Snallygasters were known to fly at night, raiding barns, pastures, and chicken coops. They even attacked small, unattended children. Snallygasters also crept into homes during the day and stole a small household item. Later, they would return the item, but in an out-of-the-way place. It was not uncommon for hunters to see them on South Mountain from Frederick to Harpers Ferry.

The number seven warded off the Snallygaster. Thus, by far, the best protection was to paint a seven-pointed star on the largest barn on the property. It had to be precisely laid out, or it would not work. In its early days, horror stories of the Snallygaster were passed along by word of mouth, explanations for missing children or chickens or huge creatures seen in the sky. Not only was the creature's name modified over the years, so too did its appearance change and morph. The Snallygaster, as it came to be known, transformed from its original half-ghoul and half-bird with massive wings, a thick, bloodsucking beak, and flesh-piercing talons to a half-bird and half-reptile. By the turn of the century, the beak had become elongated and metallic, and it had gained razor-sharp teeth and a twenty-foot wingspan. Some descriptions even added that this creature had octopus tentacles protruding from the mouth.

In January 1908, a Hagerstown Mail reporter related that a hiker in the Quirauk Mountain area, the highest point on South Mountain, happed upon a wild bird he had never seen.

The feathered, bird-like creature with eyes like balls of fire was making a nest in the rocks. Its beak measured at least six inches and had rows of saw-like teeth on the upper and lower bill. The neck spanned at least two feet. The feathers were sheening silver, gold-like bristles, and sparkled like diamonds. The weight was approximately seventy-five pounds. It flew past the man giving an unearthly shriek. Bullets shot at the bird did not seem to penetrate the body.

*Quirauk Mountain-where the story of the huge, bird-like creature took flight. **High Rock Overlook**, 14237 Pen Mar High Rock Road, Highfield-Cascade, MD 21719 (39.694979, -77.523446)*

In 1909 and after more sightings, Middletown Valley Register editor George Rhoderick and reporter Ralph Wolfe, seeking new readers for the newspaper, flew with the story using a twist on the local German folklore of the Snallygaster. A series of outrageous stories from Ohio to Virginia surrounding the fictional Snallygaster-ish creature were doled out to the public. It had "enormous wings, a long pointed bill, claws like steel hooks, and an eye in the center of its forehead." It made a sound like a loud locomotive whistle. More reports began popping up of winged monsters flying around the mountains. No one would know which stories were from genuine witnesses and which were faked. The articles eventually faded into the news archives.

The Middletown Valley Register used the old legend of the Snallygaster in a hoax to get readers in the 1900s.

Even after the truth was leaked, the creature was given a new breath of life when citizens revived its story twenty-three years later in the 1930s. Charles Main, Middletown resident and ice cream dealer, scoffed at those who turned their noses up at the validity of the creature when he happed upon it in the autumn of 1932. "People who say there is no such animal are the ones who need to get it right. We are not. I saw the Snallygaster, and I saw him change from white to black." He and another man were returning from Frederick to Middletown on Tuesday, November 22nd, 1932, when a winged creature swept up from the south about 25 feet in the air near the old John Hagan's Tavern (5018 Old National Pike, Braddock Heights). It appeared to have streamers coming from its mouth like an octopus's arms, and the wingspan was about 14 feet. Much to their relief, it turned before it got to them. Two boys would support Main's claims, stating that they saw a creature flying towards Middletown from South Mountain.

John Hagan's Tavern.

Braddock Heights —*where several witnesses saw what appeared to be a creature with a wingspan about 12 to 14 feet and streamers coming from its mouth like the arms of an octopus.*

As the stories gained momentum, so did public fear. Streets were vacant of children at dusk. Adults feared going outside after dark; doors were locked and windows were bolted shut. Thus, in December of 1932, local newspapers decided to put an end to all the reports. Writers pronounced the beast's death, reporting it had gotten attracted to the scent of alcohol in the Frog Hollow section of Washington County. It appeared to have lost all control of its wings and fell into a giant vat. It was nothing but bones by the time the police found it.

Regardless, the Snallygaster still lived. A couple driving from Frederick to Buckeystown the previous month (November 1932) recalled passing Mt. Olivet cemetery around 5:30 p.m., and just over the rise was a dark, bulky, and winged figure they quickly identified as a Snallygaster. The car nearly swerved off the road as the beast whipped out a wing into their path.

Mt Olivet Cemetery—nearby, a couple nearly hit a Snallygaster with their car.

In a village called Monkeytown in West Virginia, during March of 1935, the Snallygaster terrorized the Bland family, treeing the father. In May, the Snallygaster had moved nearly 70 miles north to Hopewell, where witnesses watched it spew poisonous vapor.

It is many years later, and there are not many new stories to tell of the Snallygaster. But surely, the creature lives on. It has withstood the test of time of nearly three-hundred years. Old-timers have passed down that when the Snallygaster lays an egg, it takes twenty long years to hatch. Perhaps we need to be patient, sit back, and wait for the next generation to send terror into our hearts.

Where else can you look for the Snallygaster?

Along the Towpath Trail. The Snallygaster has been known to live in caves near South Mountain since early Germans settled there. While not unique to West Virginia, its range is quite extensive. Major overlooks like Weverton Cliffs just outside Harpers Ferry are great places to watch for winged creatures.

Weverton Cliffs (South Mountain) Along the Appalachian Trail, Knoxville, MD 21758 (39.333424, -77.676774)

Weverton Cliffs Parking Lot—Weverton Cliffs Road, Knoxville, MD 21758 (39.333157, -77.683358) Tip of South Mountain. Park and head 400 feet southeast on Weverton Cliff Road to Appalachian Trail at the end of the road. Appalachian Trail—704 Weverton Road Knoxville, MD 21758 (39.332781, -77.682179)

*You can also hike the **Chesapeake and Ohio Towpath Trail** just across the Potomac River from Harpers Ferry. It will lead you toward the area of Frog Hollow where the Snallygaster came to its alleged end—or perhaps not. **Maryland Heights Trail Parking-Towpath Trail** is right across Harpers Ferry Road. (limited parking, but you can also park in Harpers Ferry and walk the bridge to the towpath) 613-699 Harpers Ferry Road, Knoxville, MD 21758 (39.330763, -77.734370)*

*Take about an 18-mile drive along **Old National Pike and US-40 ALT W from Frederick** (39.414299, -77.410625) past Braddock Heights and Middletown and over South Mountain to Boonsboro (39.506349, -77.652418). You'll pass many of the places the Snallygaster was known to roam.*

Maryland

Dwayyo

Bushy-tailed Dogman

Description: Wolf-like. Big as a bear. Dark. 6-foot tall. Long, bushy tail. Built like a dog. Walks upright.

Other Names: Wolf-dog. Dogman.

Location: Ellerton, MD, West Middletown, MD Gambrill State Park -Frederick, MD—Frederick County and Sykesville, MD—Carroll County

Near Rock Run Campground— Gambrill State Park.

The mysterious Dwayyo pops up in the vicinity of Frederick County in Maryland and seems to prefer wild areas like Gambrill Park. However, with a background that appears to be wolf or coyote-like, it may hap upon a suburban or rural lawn once in a while foraging for food. Coyotes will eat whatever is available—a deer carcass lying on the road or even the occasional stray cat. Both calves, cats, and dogs have come up missing whenever Dwayyos are around.

The Dwayyo is a six-foot-tall bear-sized creature walking upright but built like a dog. It has a long and bushy tail. There were sightings of huge footprints and horrible yowls in Frederick County in 1944 connected to the Dwayyo. The wolf-like beast was quiet for twenty years. In November of 1965, a man going by John Becker, who lived near Gambrill State Park, told police that he went out into his yard as darkness was falling to search out the identity of a strange noise. After a thorough investigation and finding no cause for the sound, he turned back toward his house. At that moment, Becker noticed in horror that there was something large and dark lunging toward him. It stood upright on its hind legs. It was as big as a bear with long black hair and a bushy tail. Becker fought off the attacker until it escaped into the woods. Afterward, he contacted authorities—anonymously. The idea some wolf-like beast had attacked him seemed ludicrous at best.

Becker's identity, being unknown, made the story appear somewhat sketchy. However, on December 7th, 1965, a woman in Jefferson about ten miles away complained a large animal shaped like a dog was harassing her cows. It was as big as a calf. In the summer of 1966, and on Gambrill State Park's outskirts, a camper happened upon a shaggy, two-legged beast. It was as large as a deer with a triangular-shaped head and pointy ears. It was dark brown and screamed when approached, retreating in a remarkable walk—spiderlike as its legs stuck out from the body. In June of 1973, police in Sykesville called in helicopters and a search crew when Anthony Norris reported finding footprints 13 1/2 inches long and 6 inches wide. Other residents described seeing a hairy beast that was seven to ten feet tall with a bushy tail and dark hair. Some reported cows and dogs killed. Others thought this elusive beast might be a mix between a Snallygaster and a Dwayyo.

About seven miles away in Ellerton, a woman reported hearing beastly screams and cries in the mountains for months. A search of the areas by police failed to turn up clues. In the autumn of 1976, there was another sighting when two men were driving an off-road near Route 77 between Cunningham Falls State Park and Catoctin Mountain National Park, spotlighting deer populations with their vehicle headlights for the upcoming hunting season. (It is illegal to do this now.) Instead of finding deer, the two saw a large wolf-like creature dart in front of their car. The description was a canine-like head, hyena-like banded fur, and the creature walked hunched and in an upright position on muscled legs. In 1978, two park rangers would see the same type of animal near Cunningham Falls.

The Dwayyo's greatest enemy is the half-bird and half-reptile Snallygaster. More elusive than the Snallygaster, it does appear to have the same range. No one has ever been able to capture the creature physically. Reports and verbal eye-witness accounts are the only forms of evidence.

Where else can you look for the Dwayyo?

*Gambrill State Park Frederick County Maryland
(39.472057, -77.494403)*

Gambrill State Park, near the location of Becker's attack in 1965, offers more than a few trails with overlooks to search for the Dwayyo. Gambrill Park is located on Catoctin Mountain near the city of Frederick and is known for its views, including those from High Knob. No, you can't spotlight for deer or any beast or animal!

South Frederick Overlook at Gambrill State Park
*8602 Gambrill Park Road, Middletown, MD 21769
(39.463939, -77.494670)*

North Frederick Overlook
*Gambrill Park Road, Frederick, MD 21702
(39.469986, -77.494523)*

Sykesville Monster

Close Encounter with an Ape-Man

Maryland

Description: 7-8 feet tall. Hairy. Dark. Ape-like.

Other Names: Bigfoot. Ape-Man.

Location: Sykesville, MD—Carroll County

It would be just another mundane spring morning of fly-fishing for smallmouth and redeye bass on May 9th, 1981, if Lon Strickler had not chosen to fish along the South Branch of the Patapsco River not far from River Road in Sykesville.

It was a riffle-pool Strickler had set his sights on, so with his pole in hand and waders on feet, he treaded out on to the water and prepared for a relaxing morning of fishing. Half-heartedly, he noticed a stray dog moseying around the brush of the bank but was too focused on the task at hand to take much heed. Moments later, his attention was caught by a peculiar, deep growling followed by a dog's frightened yapping. Strickler towed his attention from his fishing and looked up just as the dog's barking came to an abrupt halt. There was a short, resounding yelp. And he was shocked to see a huge—seven to eight feet tall—creature with dark, matted hair nearly hidden in the bushes on the bank. *Tick-tick*—was the sound it made as it ambled from the brush and toward the forest beyond. The reek that followed was nearly overwhelming—musky and intensely bitter like that of fox urine.

Strickler immediately contacted local authorities of his sighting. He had passed the dog on his way out, noting it was bloody but only slightly injured. He thought it strange that Maryland State Police and the Feds would be the ones to follow-up on his finding. Oddly, the authorities forced him to leave the scene, and they refused to offer information about the mysterious event later.

There would be others who maintained they either saw this Bigfoot-like creature or caught sight of the massive footprints. In 1993, an eight-year-old boy in Woodstock reported seeing the monsters. Along Piney Run in Marriottsville, a fisherman happened upon a pile of ape-like fur with bones appearing much like a human's skeletal frame, including a skull. Local authorities were contacted and came quickly to the scene, along with helicopters and unmarked vehicles. There was no mention of the incident afterward, which has fueled the fire for many who are sure there was a coverup of the strange confrontation.

Where else can you look for the Sykesville Monster?

Hugg-Thomas Wildlife Management Area—*Sykesville. The South Branch of the Patapsco River runs through this forested area, then parallels River Road just past Sykesville Road (Route 32) where there have been sightings.*

It is also near Schoolhouse Road and Norris Avenue where according to Sykesville police chief Omer Herbert, three human-like footprints measuring 13 1/2-inches long and almost 6-inches wide were found in June of 1973 during the Dwayyo scare.

Hugg Thomas Wildlife Management Area: 13205 Forsythe Road, Sykesville, MD 21784 Parking (39.358515, -76.973737)

Maryland

Goatman

Goatman of Fletchertown Road

Description: Hairy. Walks upright on two legs. Half-man and half-goat.

Other Names: Abominable Phantom.

Location: Bowie, MD—Prince George's County

The Goatman on Fletchertown Road in Bowie. He is described as hairy, walking upright on two legs, and half-man, half-goat. Take a drive along Fletchertown Road, you just might see him.

Fletchertown Road is a less-than-two-mile stretch of roadway. It is hardly secluded like it used to be in the 1970s.

Those were the years when Eleanor Roosevelt High, Bowie High, Parkdale High, and DuVal High School teens made their rite of passage trips along the lonesome pot-hole ridden, asphalt-buckled street. Their mission was to search out the elusive Goatman prowling the isolated patch of roadway and surrounding area. Now the road is freshly asphalted with pockets of woodland and the remoteness has been shoved aside for busy subdivisions with newer homes and the constant sound of traffic driving through. The old GOATMAN WAS HERE scrawls of black spray paint on dumped refrigerators, and worn plywood tacked to fences that used to be there are long gone. But it is not to say that the Goatman and those who seek him out are displaced or departed. Some believe he is still there just like he has been since their moms and dads, grandmas and grandpas searched him out some fifty years ago.

Him. *The Goatman.* He might have been the spawn of some mad scientist from nearby Beltsville Agricultural Research Center whose experiments on goats in the 1970s went awry. He mutated into a half-human and half-goat himself. Or he could be the cranky and hairy old hermit living in a shack in the woods and known to walk the Penn Central Railroad tracks wielding an ax and who liked to scare pesky kids away. Or maybe, he could be a beady-eyed Bigfoot creature lurking the backstreets. Whatever this monster was or still is depends upon with whom you speak. What we do know is that it gave thrill-seeking high schoolers something to do on Friday and Saturday nights and scared the bejeebus out of more than a few people in its heyday. Take April Edwards, for example. It would have been a typical Wednesday night—November 3rd, 1971—if not for the sixteen-year-old Old Bowie resident coming face to face with the creature in her yard where it nearly abutted the railroad tracks on Zug Road.

"I had seen it on the night in question," April would relate. "It just looked like a hairy man to me. It was on two legs and stood upright, though it did crouch over when it ran, like a hunchback. It had long hair, and I don't think it was part-this or part-that, I think it was human." The same night, her beloved ten-month-old German Shepherd-mix, Ginger, disappeared. Knowing she was upset, neighborhood folks went out looking for the pet.

Fletchertown Road in Bowie.

Twenty-year-old Willie Gheen was living with April's family. He and his neighbor, twenty-year-old John Hayden, grabbed up a couple of bats and ventured out. They made a gruesome discovery of the dog's decapitated head on the frosted grass. Hayden had also caught the image of the creature, and he recalled, "It was an animal. It was about six-foot, something like that, and hairy, like an animal. As far as I know, it was an animal on two feet. I remember it made a high-pitched sound like a squeal." No one found Ginger's body. Other pets disappeared suspiciously in the area. April Edwards recounted seeing the man-like creature two weeks later near Hayden's junkyard and towing business. "—the second time it was looking for food or something," she said.

"This thing was for real—this was not folklore. I do not know what it was. Whatever it was, I believe it killed my dog and was living in the woods around there for some time."

It was not the first time a creature was in the region. On August 1st, 1957, a couple living about sixteen miles from the location where April's dog was killed had a horrifying experience. The Garners of Upper Marlboro pulled into their driveway and were quite frightened by a hairy, gorilla-like creature with red, beady eyes in their path. It was walking upright. Mister Garner slowed his vehicle with a quick push of foot on the brake but still struck the creature lightly. So shocked was the man, he backed up his car quickly only to find the enraged beast in hot pursuit! It was called the *Abominable Phantom* in newspapers. Authorities organized a hunt, but search parties found no clues to the encounter.

If the stories have dwindled over the years, it may not be for lack of the creature. Like many people in bustling communities, folks tend to focus on getting from Point A to Point B. They just might not be looking. During my drive-through to take in the stomping grounds of the elusive Goatman, I passed through the town of Frederick. My cell phone started screaming a warning to find safety—the weather service caught a tornado on the radar. I looked up, and sure enough, the clouds were churning and twisting a tornado right above my jeep. And yet, all around me, everyone was going about their day—kids were playing on the sidewalks, cars were speeding to their next destination, people were out on their porches chatting mildly. They did not even notice the three fingerlings of tornados spiraling on the horizon or the one forming above their homes. So maybe we are simply not focused. Or with the encroachment of pricy homes along the Goatman's old stomping grounds, he may have moved to more secluded stretches of land around Prince George's County.

Where can you look for the Goatman?

Most of the area is filled with homes now, but there are little pockets of natural areas around Bowie for those entertaining the idea of searching Goatman out, including:

Northridge Park—12227-12321 Fletchertown Road, Bowie, MD 20720 (38.991443, -76.791416)

Washington, Baltimore, and Annapolis Trail—WB & A Trail (Along with the Bowie Heritage Trail) (39.009692, -76.746399)

Washington, Baltimore and Annapolis Trail

If you like urban legends, do not forget about the Governor's Bridge between Bowie and Davidsonville. More

Governor's Bridge over the Patuxent River—Governor Bridge Road, Bowie, MD 20716 (38.951466, -76.6935050)

than a few passersby have listened to the sorrowful wail of a newborn baby under this Crybaby Bridge, the grievous ending left over after a woman tossed her infant from the bridge.

Maryland

Chesapeake Bay Chessie

Sea Serpent in Chesapeake Bay

Description: 20 - 40 feet tall. Serpent-like. Swims moving snake-like up and down or side to side in the water.

Other Names: Sea Serpent. Bay Monster.

Location: Chesapeake Bay—Maryland and Virginia

The first reported sighting of Chessie may have been in 1846 when the Schooner Empire had a close encounter.

There is a mysterious monster in the Chesapeake Bay. People have seen it, including Robert and Karen Frew, who live on Love Point on Kent Island. On a clear night in May of 1982, Robert saw what appeared to be a thirty-foot, log-like creature moving against the tide. He recorded a three-minute color video of the snake-like creature that viewers fondly dubbed Chessie.

"I would say thirty to thirty-five feet would be about right," Robert Frew described the sea monster. "It's about the size of a good-sized person's thigh—about ten inches in diameter." The body appeared to have humps. He also suggested that its head was rounder than a football and close to that of a snake. Smithsonian Institution scientists reported that the film appeared to be authentic. However, they refused to identify the subject. The Freys were not alone in seeing Chessie. Dozens on the island saw it.

Chesapeake Bay.

It was not the first time people have spotted serpents in the Chesapeake Bay. The February 27th, 1846 American Republican and Baltimore Daily Clipper newspaper reported that Captain Lawson of the Schooner Empire felt his vessel drag across something substantial near the mouth of the Chesapeake Bay. He assumed that it was the rusty mast pole of an old wrecked ship since it was dark in color. However, as the schooner passed over, whatever had rubbed against the hull was *moving*. Upon further inspection, the captain and the crew recognized with alarm, not just one but two distinct heads and bodies and mouths marked in reddish hues at the jawlines were jutting out from the bay water.

They were sea serpents! The first raised out of the water at least ten to twelve feet with a sixty-foot body that was the circumference of a ship's mast.

As years passed, there were other sightings:

—The New Orleans Republican, on August 16th, 1876, reported that witnesses saw a sea serpent in the Chesapeake Bay. It was twenty-five feet long and as thick as a flour barrel.

—June 7th, 1934, two men fishing in the bay—Francis Klarman and Edward Ward—spotted the serpent sidling up to the side of their boat. It was black and about twelve feet long with a skull the size of a football and shaped like a horse's head. It dove into the water. Then, it disappeared.

—There were a rash of sightings in 1978 and then in the early 1980s. In 1980, Helen Jones got a close look at the creature while she was crabbing—close enough to touch, that is. She watched in awe as it came up out of the water. Helen described it as: "round as a watermelon, more brownish than gray and had white spots on the hump."

It appears most of the witnesses describe Chesapeake Bay Chessie as being twenty-five to forty feet long, snake-like, swimming in an undulating motion—side to side. It is much larger than a manatee or shark, which some have speculated could be the mysterious creature's identity.

Where can you look for Chessie?

Sandy Point State Park is just across the bay from Kent Island. It is a great place to Chessie Watch. Grab up a lawn chair and binoculars, head on out to the beach, and see what kind of sea serpent you can find!

Sandy Point State Park —Anne Arundel County

1100 E College Parkway

Annapolis, MD 21409 (39.014463, -76.399732)

The Monsters of West Virginia

Monster/Cryptid	Map #	Monster/Cryptid	Map #
Snarly Yow	1	Giant Bird	17
Snallygaster	2	Grant Town Goon	18
Hellhound	3	Wendigo	19
Appalachian Chupacabra	4	Bigfoot—	
Tommyknockers	5	*Flatwoods/Sutton — Bigfoot*	20
Flatwoods Monster	6	*Monongahela Richwood— Yahoo*	21
Mothman	7	*Marlinton —Apple Devil*	22
Sheepsquatch	8	*Blackwater Falls—Bigfoot*	23
Flying Ray	9	*Canaan Valley National Wildlife Refuge —Bigfoot*	24
Wampus Cat	10	*New River Gorge— Bigfoot*	25
White Thing/Veggie Man	11	*Webster County—The Hairy One*	26
Grafton Monster	12	*Monongahela National Forest—Yellow Gape*	27
Ogua	13	*Polk Gap/Poke Holler Monster*	28
Ohio River Monster	14	*Seneca Rocks—Ghillie Beast*	29
Cumberland Dragon	15		
Marrtown Banshee	16		

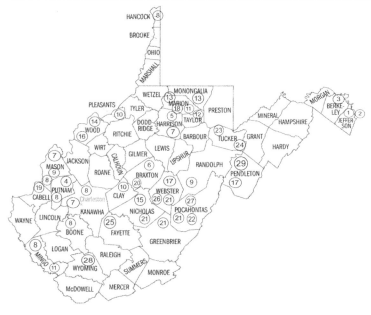

West Virginia

Hellhound

Black Dogs in Martinsburg

Description: Glowing red eyes. Dark in color. Black bear-size—larger and bulkier than a normal dog.

Other Names: Black Dog.

Location: Martinsburg, WV—Berkeley County

Hellhounds were seen along the roads near Green Hill Cemetery.

It was the autumn of 1873, October, to be more precise. It was not long after the beaten corpse of twelve-year-old Annie Butler was found in Cunningham Woods in Little Georgetown ten miles from Martinsburg, West Virginia.

John Taliaferro was arrested for the murder and convicted of his crime the next summer. Not long after, he was taken by an angry mob at midnight on Thursday, August 13th, 1874, from the Berkeley County Jail in Martinsburg.

Men forced their way into the building where he was being held and placed him into a one-horse wagon. The crowd marched beside it cheering from King Street to Burke Street, High Street to Williamsport Pike. They stopped at Warm Spring Avenue, where the railroad crossed its path, placed a sturdy rope around an oak tree limb, and hung the man. His body was placed in a wooden box and left on the side of the road at Green Hill Cemetery in hopes a family member would bury him. No one did. Someone finally buried the rotting corpse outside the cemetery in a gully along the road.

That was when the dogs began to show up along East Burke Street and to the cemetery. They were as big as calves and pitch black. Their eyes lit up a peculiar blood red. An Irishman came upon the beasts near the bridge where the crowd lynched Taliaferro. Ghostly, they were, and not of the canine flesh. So scared was the man, he ran away. Many would see these phantom dogs, and they were convinced that the creatures were Hellhounds, while others said the criminal had come back in the form of one of these phantom dogs as a curse for murdering the young girl.

Where else can you look for the Hellhounds (although I would suspect you should avoid them at all costs)?

The Hellhounds were seen running along Warm Springs Avenue where Taliaferro was hung and all the way up to Burke Street where Taliaferro's body was dumped and then past Green Hill Cemetery.

Green Hill Cemetery and East Burke Street
486 East Burke Street
Martinsburg, WV 25404
(39.455170, -77.955658)

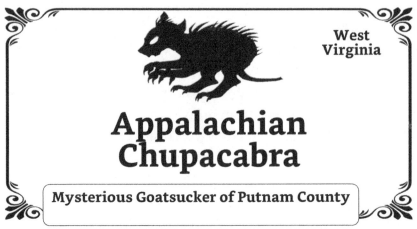

Appalachian Chupacabra

West Virginia

Mysterious Goatsucker of Putnam County

Description: Peach-fuzz fur. Pig-like snout. A layer of spike-like hackles along the back. Sharp teeth with fangs. Stands 3-4 feet high.

Other Names: Goatsucker. West Virginia Vampire.

Location: Putnam County, WV

Along WV-62 (Charleston Road) in Putnam County is as good a place as any to start on your quest for this elusive creature.

Most common in southern Americas, this version of the Chupacabra has migrated northward to the lesser populated regions of West Virginia. It has brown peach-fuzz fur, a pig-like snout, and a layer of spike-like hackles along the spine.

It has sharp teeth with fangs, and stands three to four feet high. The Appalachian Chupacabra has three toes on each foot that appear more like hawk talons than dog nails. These creatures are notoriously known for taking down their prey—chickens, sheep, goats, or deer and sucking the animal clean of any blood. When excited, they let out a high-pitched scream.

Where can you look for the Chupacabra?

Searching out this secretive little creature is like trying to find a needle in a haystack because of its wide range. So, the best thing to do is take a drive along roadways like WV-62. It is the perfect habitat for coyotes who share the same scavenger-predator habits as the Chupacabra. Look for places with roads offering plenty of road-kill deer, rabbits, and raccoons on the highway, along with small farms to steal a chicken or two once in a while. One thing to watch for if you are trying to find the Chupacabra—keep an eye on local newspapers. Pay close attention to high numbers of missing pets in specific areas and reports of animals (especially cats and dogs) who have been found dead with mysterious teeny holes in their bodies—a sure sign that a Chupacabra may be lurking around.

Other remote areas like the Guyandotte River in Lincoln County, near Piney Bottoms, offer the perfect habitat for Chupacabra.

West Virginia

Tommyknocker

Tricksters of Brandy Gap Tunnel

Description: 2-3 feet tall. Wrinkled face with bristly whiskers. Wiry with long arms, short legs. Wears miner clothing. Known to play tricks like stealing miners' tools and food from lunch pails. Knocks on walls before slate and rock falls, but will sometimes knock to taunt the miners (or now hikers) in tunnels and caves.

Other Names: Fairy. The Knocker.

Location: Salem, WV—Harrison County

Tommyknocker inside the famous Brandy Gap Tunnel #2 .

There are creatures in the dark depths of Brandy Gap Tunnel #2 near Salem. They seem to thrive in the dank darkness, flourishing in the mixture of slimy sludge dribbling from the rotting wood of the caskets and long-dead bodies from the cemetery above. Oldtimers call them Tommyknockers, a mischievous lot and a bit of a wildcard when it comes to interacting with humans. It depends upon their mood whether they taunt those within their lair or save them from some catastrophe.

The railroad path that disrupts its den was once a part of the Northwestern Virginia Railroad for the Baltimore and Ohio and served as a connection between Grafton and Parkersburg. Now the tracks are gone just like the miners who brought a Tommyknocker or two there when they dug through the hill to clear the path for the railway. But the creatures still live on inside. Some believe that the eerie voices, sobbing, and chatter heard within the tunnel are attributed to the ghostly remains of those buried at the Enon Baptist Church Cemetery above. Others suggest it could be those old Tommyknockers up to their pranks again.

Brandy Gap Tunnel #2 (Flinderation Tunnel). Be wary when visiting areas with Tommyknockers. They are known to "borrow" things!

When laborers were digging through the mountain from 1852 to 1857, they reported strange lights and odd sounds inside the tunnel. They also heard the *knock-knock-knock* of the spirited little Tommyknockers. Those pesky little characters played pranks on the miners and tunnel builders while they worked, like stealing their lunches right out of their pails and tossing pebbles at them. However, they also warned them of falling rocks with their signature rap on the walls. Sometimes. Not always. More often than not. And certainly not on Saturdays when the Tommyknockers took the day off.

It is not hard to imagine all sorts of creepy things inside on a stormy day in shin-deep water and mist swirling around.

When the workers were tunneling through Brandy Gap, a certain amount of superstition was involved with digging so close to the little church cemetery on the hillside above. But Saturdays were the worst days for accidents—legends say Tommyknockers are known to take that specific day off. Therefore, the men were probably already jumpy one cold, snowy Saturday of January 15th of 1853—there were no Tommyknockers on duty to give them a rock-fall heads-up.

Their fears were warranted because a man died by a fall of rock on that day. The Cooper's Clarksburg Register wrote this: *Killed. A man named Hanley was killed at the Brandy Gap Tunnel on last Saturday by a quantity of earth falling on him. He was taken to Fairmont, on Monday, for interment. Two other men were seriously injured.*

It is safe to say the miners heard *knock-knock* warnings of Tommyknocker knuckles to a wall after that because no others were known to be killed by falling rock at the tunnel while being built either on the weekdays—or on Saturdays. That said, you can walk the tunnel. It is along the West Virginia Rail Trail. But if you hear any *knock-knock-knocking*, GET OUT! And perhaps hike on a weekday.

Where can you look for Tommyknockers?

You can walk the North Bend Rail Trail through Brandy Gap Tunnel #2 (also called Flinderation Tunnel). It is a short hike to the tunnel. Bring a flashlight, umbrella, and boots if it is raining. The water inside fills up along the path, and it drips from the roof!

North Bend Rail-Trail—Just off Northwestern Pike (US 50) on to Pine Valley/Tunnel Drive. The tunnel is .3 miles (about a six-minute walk) from the parking area.

Pine Valley Drive, Salem, WV 26426

(39.290304, -80.498480)

There is also parking on the opposite side: (about .1 miles or a two-minute walk)

Flinderation Road, Salem, WV 26426

(39.294231, -80.509843)

West
Virginia

Flatwoods Monster

Flatwoods-Home of the Green Monster

Description: 8-10 feet tall. Man-like but not human—more like a machine. Dark green, glowing with a round, blood-red face surrounded by a pointed, hooded shape. Two eyes with light beams.

Other Names: Green Monster. Braxton County Monster.

Location: Flatwoods, WV—Braxton County

Deep in the autumn of 1952, something came to Flatwoods, West Virginia—spiraling out of the sky in a great ball of fire.

It captured front pages of newspapers across the nation in the autumn of 1952, the bizarre experience of a Flatwoods mother along with her two sons, a teen National Guardsman, a handful of neighbor children, and a few dogs.

It played out like the classic science fiction movies popular in theatres at its time. But this story was not some comic-book-style flick hatched in a Hollywood film-maker's mind. It was real.

The boys took off from the playground (where the school is now) toward the hill, down Main Street, up Depot Street, and to the farm.

It was 7:15 p.m. on Friday, September 12th, 1952. A group of boys were playing football at the local Flatwoods Elementary School, among them brothers Edison May (age 13) and Freddie May (age 11). As the afternoon ebbed toward a dusky evening, an eerie silence interrupted their game. One of the boys called out: "Look there!" Above them, a silver-red ball of fire with flames trailing behind swept across the sky barely above the trees. They watched in wonder as this object, described as "bigger than the average aircraft," slowed. It tilted upward and appeared to sink gradually, landing on a flattened hilltop to the southeast— by a cistern at the property of local farmer, G. Bailey Fisher.

They were overcome with curiosity believing it was a meteorite or a flying saucer, and raced down the streets in pursuit. As they crested the road where the odd object landed, the boys came to the home of Edison and Freddie.

They burst through the doors in a flurry to tell the adults what they had seen. Their mother, Kathleen May, had just gotten off work at a beauty parlor in nearby Sutton. Not wanting the boys to explore the strange site alone but still in her work uniform, she snatched up a flashlight resting on the coffee table and followed.

The Monster Stood right on the spot where Mrs. Kathleen May and these six boys pose for the photographer, according to their stories. Shown are Mrs. May, her two sons, Edward and Theodore, and Eugene Lemon, Ronald Shaver, Theodore Neal and Neal Nunley, all of Flatwoods. They're standing pat on their story that they saw a huge green monster on this spot Friday night following the flight of a meteorite through West Virginia skies. (Staff Photo)

The witnesses: Kathleen May, her two sons Edison and Freddie and Eugene Lemon, Ronald Shaver, Teddie Neal, Neil Nunley, and Tommy Hyer standing on the spot where they saw the monster. Image: Flatwoods Monster Museum.

Some of the original boys who saw the flaming ball at the football field would turn around, go back home. Still, several neighborhood children tagged along with Edison, Freddie, and their mother, including six-year-old Tommy Hyer and fourteen-year-olds Ronald Shaver, Teddie Neal, and Neil Nunley. When eighteen-year-old National Guardsman Gene Lemon heard the boys' commotion at the home, he would join the adventure. His mother had been drinking a cup of coffee with a friend. When the object flew past, it shook the house so heartily that their coffees spilled on the table.

Lemon grabbed up a flashlight and accompanied the group along with his dog. Freddie May's dog, Ricky, and another neighborhood pup scampered by their side. It was a little past 7:40 p.m. when the eight walked through one field along an old road path where they saw a flashing light. Eugene led the group with Neil by his side. Behind the two were Kathleen and Edison, followed by Ronald. Freddie, Teddie, and Tommy lagged behind, stopping at a wood fence while the rest continued onward.

At some point along the trail, the air filled with fog and a mist with a metallic, sulfur-like stench burning their nostrils, throat, and eyes. About a hundred yards from where the five who continued were approaching, Kathleen May instantly noted a massive ball of fire about ten feet in diameter and a light that pulsated with strange hissing, popping, and crackling sounds. A whirring noise like a generator echoed in the air. Gene Lemon whipped up his flashlight to take in a tall, dark green man-like figure. It had a round, reddish face that was surrounded by a pointed, hood-like shape.

It was a ten-foot monster with a blood-red face and green body descending upon the town of Flatwoods in 1952.

The eyes were like light beams wavering. "I saw a pair of eyes near a tree and threw my flashlight on them," Eugene would later relate. "I thought it was an opossum. Then there stood this—thing." He described it as a ten-foot monster with a blood-red face and a green body that seemed to glow. Coming out what appeared to be glass on its head were fixed beams.

One dog growled and disappeared into the mist. When Kathleen May drew up her flashlight and let the light shine on the object before them, she heard the other barking violently. The group stared aghast at the towering figure while it lit up like a Christmas tree and glided over about a foot or two above the ground and to within ten feet of Kathleen May and Gene Lemon. In utter horror, Gene Lemon fell while an oily liquid squirted at them. Terrified, the feet of the group seemed nailed to the ground. Then suddenly, they all bolted, running away and back down the hillside.

THE MONSTER which prowled the hills of Braxton County on Friday, Sept. 12, was drawn by a New York artist from descriptions given him by Mrs. Kathleen May and

Kathleen May and Eugene Lemon holding up the image of the monster. It would be known as the Green Monster, the Braxton County Monster, and the Flatwoods Monster.
Image: Flatwoods Monster Museum.

Newspapers would cover the bizarre happening, but no one could ever pinpoint what the group saw that evening—a monster, an alien—? Many witnesses stepped forward to state they saw several unidentified flying craft speeding across West Virginia skies on that day. Whatever came tearing across the sky shook homes and left people both terrified and mystified in its wake.

Not all things may be explained, but they can be explored. There is a Flatwoods Monster Museum in Sutton where you can find out more information and learn some unique things about the event. And maybe while you are driving around the area, you will run into the monster-alien thing too!

Where can you look for the Flatwoods Monster?

-**Braxton County Convention & Visitor's Bureau/ Flatwoods Monster Museum**—208 Main Street, Sutton, WV 26601 (38.664529, -80.709152)

-Lot along Stonewall Jackson Highway, Flatwoods, WV. You can peer toward the area of the sighting (on private property) (38.717478, -80.657244)

Andrew Smith, Executive Director Braxton County CVB & Flatwoods Monster Museum with the original drawing of the Flatwoods Monster commissioned by Lee Steward/drawn by a New York sketch artist based on Kathleen May's description.

West
Virginia

Mothman

The Mason County Monster

Description: 6 to 7- feet tall with wings on its back. Light grey. Red eyes about 2 inches in diameter and 6 to 8 inches apart.

Other Names: Mason County Monster. Red Bird Man.

Location: Clendenin, WV—Kanawha Co; Salem, WV—Harrison Co; Point Pleasant WV—Mason Co; Gallipolis, Oh—Gallia Co

A curious monster terrorized Point Pleasant in 1966.

On Saturday, November 12th, 1966, four men helped Kanawha County resident Kenneth Duncan dig a grave in a Clendenin cemetery for his father-in-law, Homer Smith.

The cemetery outside Clendenin where the first sighting of the Mothman occurred hovering above the hillside.

Duncan looked up, saw something above the trees that "looked like a brown human being" flying overhead. Although the other men did not see the creature, Duncan's eyes were peeled to the sight. Immediately, he knew it was no bird. It was like a man with wings. "It was gliding through the trees and was in sight for about a minute," Duncan would divulge about the bizarre sighting.

It would be the earliest recorded spotting of the creature called Mothman. It certainly would not be the last. Seventy miles away and around 10:30 p.m. on Tuesday, November 15th, 1966, Merle Partridge—a contractor living in Salem, West Virginia was enjoying an evening at home watching TV. That is, until his three-year-old German Shepherd, Bandit, started barking and howling oddly from his perch on the porch as if something was near a hay barn.

It was not the first strange incident happening that week. Partridge had noted no sound of insects or crickets had filled the air around the farm. It was remarkably quiet.

Moments before the dog's violent barking, Partridge had to turn his TV off because his reception was interrupted by a herringbone pattern and a loud, high-pitched whining much like the noise a generator makes when winding up. Between the two, he knew something out of the ordinary was going on. At the same time, Bandit let out another round of horrible howls and warning snarls. Partridge hastily grabbed a flashlight, pulled out his 8-millimeter shotgun, and went to the door, opening it wide.

He let the beam of flashlight scan the nearby meadow. Through the shaft of light, Partridge found himself blinking at two red lights like bicycle reflectors. Bandit's hackles rose. He bared his teeth and launched off the porch and into the darkness of the woods. The dog that had never run off before did not come home that night. Partridge would report his sighting to Sheriff George Johnson and search for the dog for weeks, but Bandit never returned.

Almost eighty-nine miles away, newlyweds Steve (age 20) and Mary Mallette (age 20) would be joyriding about seven miles from their hometown of Point Pleasant with married couple Roger (age 18) and Linda Scarberry (age 19). The area they were driving in Scarberry's beloved black 1957 Chevy was the abandoned West Virginia Ordnance Works, locally nicknamed the TNT Area. Peaking from 1942 to 1945, the TNT Area was a large complex of over eight-thousand acres used to produce and store ammunition (trinitrotoluene —TNT) during World War II. The area retained nearly a hundred igloo-like domes designed to be hidden from aerial view. These bunkers held explosives until the site closed. After, the town utilized it as a landfill. Early on, authorities discovered residual contaminants from World War II operations, and a massive pollution clean-up was begun. But back in 1966, the area was vacant and a remote hangout spot not far off Ohio River Road (WV-62), a place to show off a car and maybe drag race.

FRIGHTENED OBSERVERS—Four young Point Pleasant residents return to the spot where an unusual creature was spotted earlier this week. The married couples, Mr. and Mrs. Steve Mallette, left, and Mr. and Mrs. Roger Scarberry contend they found a "hoof-like" print in soft sand the next day. Staff Photo by

The Athens Messenger, November 18th, 1966— Four young Point Pleasant residents return to the spot where an unusual creature was spotted earlier this week. The married couples Mr. and Mrs. Steve Mallette, left, and Mr. and Mrs. Roger Scarberry contend they found a "hoof-like" print in soft sand the next day. Staff photo by George Lovell. Photo courtesy The Athens Messenger.

Igloo-like bunkers cover the old TNT Area and once held explosives. Then and now, people like to explore the vacant buildings and woods leading to them. It is part of the McClintic Wildlife Management Area and trails are accessible.

On that ill-fated evening, that is precisely what the two couples were doing when they happened upon the creature shortly before midnight. "We were riding through the TNT Area on a side road by the old powerhouse building around midnight on Tuesday, November 15th, 1966, when we came over this small rise in the road," Linda Scarberry reported to local police. "All at once, Steve yelled for us to look at that thing in the road. I looked up and saw it go around the corner at the old powerhouse. It did not run but wobbled like it couldn't keep its balance. Its wings were spread just a little. We sat there for a few seconds. Then Roger took off—"

The Powerhouse. *The winged monster with red eyes would appear at the powerhouse for the old West Virginia Ordnance to more than just the joyriding couples. Courtesy: Jeff Wamsley-Author of Mothman: Behind the Red Eyes, and Curator of Mothman Museum.*

Steve Mallette knew the local wildlife—had been an avid hunter since he was a mere six-years-old, and believed it was nothing more than a raccoon or other woodland critter. "We came over a little rise in the road out near the old power plant when we saw the eyes over in the bushes reflecting off the headlights. They glowed red and were six inches apart," he told the press. But when Roger Scarberry pulled out on to the main road, the eyes reappeared. However, this time, they could see the body attached—a man-like form with a ten-foot wingspan. "This thing stood about six-feet-tall with wings on its back." Roger described the creature. "It was light grey in color, with red eyes about two inches in diameter six to eight inches apart."

Roger Scarberry sped off toward the town of Point Pleasant. Those in the car saw it appear at a turn on the roadway near a billboard. It spread its wings and flew straight upward, then as fear chilled their bones, the creature followed above the car. "I was doing 100 to 105 miles per hour, and it was just gliding overtop, sorta moving from side to side," Scarberry revealed. "You could hear a flapping noise. Then it came down at the car, making a squealing noise like a mouse."

On the straightaway.

The turn where the billboard once stood and the couples came face to face with the creature once more.

The couples watched in horror as the creature appeared on a turn on Ohio River Road (WV-62) near a billboard. Just after is a long stretch where Scarberry pushed the car to over a 100 miles per hour as the Mothman kept steady pace with his Chevy.

Linda Scarberry disclosed that the eyes were large and fiery red, and it had a wingspan so vast, the tips were hitting the doors of the car as it hovered overhead when they raced down the straight stretch of roadway. Later, Scarberry noted the paint was scratched on the car. They continued into town and did not stop until they realized the creature was no longer in pursuit.

When the couples reached the local Dairyland, they stopped long enough to debate whether to contact the police or return to the site to see if the creature had left. Deciding the police would not believe their story, the couples started back toward the TNT area only to turn around once again out of uneasiness. They wanted to get an opinion of their terrifying experience from Gary Northrup, the owner of the local Tiny's Diner on Jackson Avenue.

They then saw the sizeable dead dog on the side of the road and near it, the creature that jumped away and headed on into a field. Later, some concluded this might have been Merle Partridge's German Shepherd. The dog's identity was never found because the carcass disappeared the same night. Mary Mallette described the reaction when they stopped at a local drive-in: "We went down by Tiny's Drive-in, and Gary and a couple of others were just coming out the door, so we told him what we had seen. We were all frightened, and the first thing he asked us was, 'Have you kids been drinking?' and our answer was, 'No, we had not been drinking.'" The two couples decided to call the police and waited there until a deputy arrived.

Each of the four witnesses related their story to Deputy Millard Halstead, who went with them back to the old building. During this time, the deputy heard a staticky sound but could not pinpoint the location it was coming. He also said he saw dust rising from a nearby coal pile but could not discern the identity. Linda Scarberry related it like this: "We sat there with our lights out for about fifteen or twenty minutes when I heard that squeaking sound like a mouse only a lot stronger. A shadow went across the building over on the hill across from us. Mary and I saw the red eyes then and told Millard. He shined the lights right on them without being told where they were. We saw dust coming from the ground or somewhere as Millard moved the spotlight around. We finally left—"

After the story reached the press, some in the community would laugh at the couples' report, each having their own idea of what they believed the creature truly was—some type of bird or a balloon. Roger Scarberry reacted with: "What this thing looked like—it is about six feet tall with large wings on its back. It has the shape of a man. It has two red eyes about two inches in diameter six to eight inches apart. A wing spread of ten feet. This thing, whatever it is, is definitely not a crane or goose or balloon or any of the things it has been called. I have seen it and know what it looks like."

More people began reporting: November 1966—Bob Bosworth and Alan Coates were riding motorcycles down Camp Conley Road (TNT Area) and decided to work their way over to the power plant. The two saw something on top of the roof of that old power plant building and stopped to check it out.

Camp Conley Road, Fairground Road, and Potters Creek Road in the area Bosworth and Coates were traveling, and Mothman was seen all lead into the wooded McClintic Wildlife Management Area. Camp Conley Road to the powerplant— (38.900658, -82.093042) to (38.923231, -82.089483)

They even tried to tilt the motorcycle so that the headlight shined on it. When that did not work, they entered the building, climbed up to the third floor, and peered across the remaining metal grating catwalks. In stunned silence, they watched as the shadowy figure walked across the catwalk toward them and eventually shot off into the night. The men would estimate its size at seven feet and the creature looked like a bird with wings folded on its back.

-November 1966—Paul Yoder and Benjamin Enoch, volunteer firefighters, called to the scene to help with traffic control during the frenzy to see Mothman, saw a bird with red eyes. The description spurned a professor to declare the creature fit the definition of a Sandhill Crane wandering off its normal migration route.

The fairgrounds now where the old powerplant was located. (38.923245, -82.089419)

The fairgrounds, left. But during the time of the Mothman sightings, the TNT powerplant and buildings were located here and all around the large property. Not far along the roadway, the creature jumped on the hood of thirteen-year-old Faye Dewitt-Leport's brother's car and stared at the rest of her siblings through the windshield. Then, it leaped to the top of the factory building. "It jumped on top the building and then just turned and sat down and crouched like a gargoyle." Faye described her entire story to author, Jeff Wamsley who put it in his book: Mothman...Behind the Red Eyes.

-November 1966— thirteen-year-old Faye Dewitt-Leport and her brothers and sisters set off in their Ford truck to see the Mothman for themselves. During the drive, the creature appeared beside the vehicle, and a terrified Faye found herself staring at it through the window even as her brother sped down the road at fifty miles per hour. After sliding to a sideways stop on one sharp turn, the monster she described as whitish and with red eyes leaped on the hood of the automobile and stared at them through the windshield. Then it bounded upward to the top of an abandoned building. Her brother immediately sprung from the truck and began tossing rocks and coal at the winged entity. The creature shot down toward the boy, and he dove back into the truck, speeding away. Mysterious men in black suits began showing up in the area, along with strange lights dotting the sky. On December 15th, 1967, the Silver Bridge at Point Pleasant collapsed. Forty-six people died—many associated the Mothman's appearance as an omen of the bridge collapse.

Where can you look for The Mothman?

You can visit the area where witnesses placed the Mothman's location. The West Virginia Ordnance Works is now a part of the McClintic Wildlife Management Area. You can walk the trails and check out the old bunkers and drive past the fairgrounds where the old north power plant was located. And you can stop off at the Mothman Museum in Point Pleasant and take in the most extensive collection of Mothman materials in the world.

Visit the Mothman Museum. Attend the Mothman Festival in September. **Mothman Museum:** *400 Main Street Point Pleasant, WV 25550 (38.842730, -82.138535)*

Explore inside an old bunker. TNT Bunker Area where Mothman was spotted:
McClintic Wildlife Management Area 1335 Potters Creek Road (2.2 miles from Route 62) West Columbia, WV 25287 Park here:
(38.932298, -82.073468)

Look for the guardrail and pull-off on right. Walk just past the pond and the first bunker is on the right.

Or . . follow the route from **Point Pleasant (WV-62)** (38.842932, -82.135431) to the **TNT area** just like those who searched out Mothman in the 1960s.
Beside the fairgrounds: (38.923226, -82.089443). Then explore the McClintic Wildlife Area.

West Virginia

Sheepsquatch

Sheepsquatch of Point Pleasant

Description: 6-10 feet tall. Thick, wooly matted white coat. Size of a brown bear. May sprint quickly on all fours or stand on two legs. Paw-like hands. Sheep head. Ram horns. The stench of sulfur surrounds it. High-pitched scream. Curled hands. Long talons.

Other Names: Sheep-Ape.

Location: Mingo, Hancock, Mason, Boone, Putnam and Kanawha counties, WV

The McClintic Wildlife Area where the elusive Sheepsquatch has been sighted.

A reality TV account of the creature comes from Kentucky where two men—Dakota Cheeks and Ricky Joyce encountered the Sheepsquatch. It was at a remote mountain property in 2004 on a weekend hunting trip—

After sleeping fitfully to strange noises and screams just outside their camper, they awakened the next morning to find one of their dogs dead. The two men jumped on their four-wheelers to investigate the weird happenings but found little until the following morning. Around 5:00 a.m., they awakened to the sound of dogs barking and something massive crashing into the camper. Loading up with weapons, they set out to find the beast. This time, they did. In a field near a cemetery, the two men discovered what Cheeks would describe as big creature—nearly nine feet tall, white, and hunched over. It had curled hands and long talons and gave gut-curling growls. Fear consumed them and the two lost their composure; Cheeks and Joyce opened fire on the white creature, then fled back to the property.

Near Point Pleasant, West Virginia, on graveled backroads better suited to all-terrain vehicles at the old TNT site (now the McClintic Wildlife Management Area), several family members worked their way home after a family reunion. The forest around them was bare. The ground was snow-covered above the gravel, forcing a tediously slow and slick drive along the backroads. As they passed one area, something rose from the side of the road. They would describe it as a creature seven to eight feet tall and covered in shaggy fur. It had legs much like a man and a face like a sheep with ram horns. They were not the only ones who witnessed the Sheepsquatch. A hunter came upon a similar animal in the same area—a goat-headed beast that had paused to take a drink from a creek. It rose and walked away.

Where can you look for Sheepsquatch?

*Along the roads and trails of **McClintic Wildlife Management Area** are ponds and thick forests where visitors have seen the shy Sheepsquatch. Like most wild animals, it appears to be non-aggressive unless provoked. So, don't irritate it. McClintic Wildlife Management Area—Potters Creek Road Point Pleasant, WV 25550 (38.932282, -82.073555)*

West Virginia

Flying Ray

Horton Horror—Stingray in the Sky

Description: Gray or orange. Smooth skin. Shaped like a manta ray, but appear translucent like a jellyfish. Wide as a car with an approximately 15-foot wingspan. Fly as if gliding in water.

Other Names: Flying Stingray. Horton Horror.

Location: Point Pleasant, WV—Mason County; Horton, WV—Randolph County

Near Ashton, West Virginia, a Flying Ray was seen between the Ohio River and WV- 2 just past the railroad tracks. (38.622998, -82.165267)

There have been sightings of a translucent flying manta ray that glides in mid-air on dry land. Eyewitnesses have watched them soar near cars on busy roadways and glide through trees in the deep woodlands. The locations they are seen are always near a waterway. Some believe it has ties to Mothman. Others think it might be a new species that scientists have yet discovered. *Perhaps.* A few of their saltwater comrades can survive in fresh water and have traveled up the Mississippi River from the gulf. In 2010, a boater found a Spiny Dogfish Shark at a ramp along the Ohio River. A May 2014 Ledger Independent story relates that fisherman John Bays found a Bull Shark almost 3-feet long at the Manchester, Ohio boat ramp on the Ohio River. At Hocking Hills State Park, quarter-sized, brainless, heartless, bloodless freshwater jellyfish swirl in the water's depths just like they do in the ocean. They are very much alive.

Regardless, people have seen Flying Ray. By Horton, West Virginia, a mother and daughter witnessed a manta-ray-shaped object fly in front of the car. The creature was dubbed The Horton Horror. And on a clear and dusky December evening around 6:00 p.m. and while driving Route 2, paralleling the Ohio River between Point Pleasant and Huntington, two witnesses observed a grayish, smooth shape swooping toward their windshield. It then vanished after heading back over the Ohio River. Could it be a genuine undiscovered freshwater ray or a mysterious cryptid? Time will only tell. Maybe you will be the one to find out.

Where can you look for the Flying Ray?

Take a drive along the scenic WV– 2 paralleling the Ohio River between Point Pleasant and Huntington and you might be lucky enough to run into one of these creatures! Oh, and do not forget when you are passing Lesage to stop in at Hillbilly Hot Dogs for a gourmet hot dog, burger, or even a vegetarian taste of West Virginia!

West Virginia

Wampus Cat

Undead Cat of King Shoals

Description: Half-mountain lion or cat and half-woman (or man, in some legends).

Other Names: Ewah. Cattywampus. Wampus Beast.

Location: Pleasants County, WV; Clay County, WV

The Wampus of Cherokee legend where a wife was condemned to walk the earth as half-mountain cat and half-woman still roams the lands of Kentucky, Tennessee, and West Virginia. And here, along old roads at Wallback Wildlife Management Area, as a being returning to right some wrong done to them.

The Wampus is fearsome as a cougar and as frightening as a phantom. This half-human and half-wildcat haunts the mountains of West Virginia, Kentucky, and Tennessee. It was not always such a formidable creature to be dreaded.

Old-timers pass down this creature was once a woman of the Cherokee. Her husband was both handsome and an excellent hunter. The woman was the suspicious type of person, always watchful, always possessive, fretting another would take her spouse. When he would leave for hunting, she would pace the floors of her home, peer through the doorway, awaiting his return. She would ask the man to reveal to her the rites he took. She would eye the other women, watching to see if any would sneak off to meet with her husband.

So mistrustful was she that one day as the men gathered in the woods to prepare for the hunt with their sacred, secret rites, she covered herself in the hide of a mountain cat and followed to spy on her husband. The men gathered around their campfire. She peered at them from the trees, taking in the stories riddled with secrets only the men could share. She watched wide-eyed at the magic the medicine man would perform.

At some point, the wife gasped in disbelief at what she overheard. The wind took her breath to the men's ears. They found her secret place and dragged her to the center of the circle. The medicine man doled out her punishment—he cast a spell on the woman, melding the mountain cat skin to her flesh and making her a strange mix of cougar and human and spirit called Ewah. She was cursed to live alone for eternity. This beast of the cursed woman makes terrifying screams at night. If she cries out, whoever hears the cry will die within three days. She steals chickens from barns and maybe a child from a bed. On nights when the wind is howling, you can see her walking upright in the darkness of the woods and hear her deathlike howls. Cherokee passed her story to traders, peddlers, and settlers who called any cougar-like beast "catamount," "cattywampus," or just plain Wampus Cat.

Along the way, the story of the Wampus Cat would yield to the legend in West Virginia of an old woman who lived alone deep in the mountains. She grew her food and tended to the sick with the medicines she would find in the forest. Folks would see her talking to herself, her hair always mussed and tangled and her clothes raggedy. Those who were wary of sorcery and demons called her a witch. When livestock began to come up missing, the fingers pointed to the eccentric old woman. They said she transformed herself into a housecat and would wait in the shadows outside the door. When someone opened the door, she would slip inside unheeded. Once inside, the witch would hide in some dark corner until those in the household fell asleep. Then she would cast an enchantment on the family so they would not awaken for the night. Once their eyes were closed tightly, she would jump out an open window and go to the barn. The old witch would mumble a spell to change from the cat to an old woman again. After that, she gathered up the livestock and took them home.

Wampus Cat of West Virginia—a witch who had the tables turned on her when she tried to outwit the townspeople with her spells.

But the townspeople caught on to her treachery. They devised a scheme to catch the old woman in the act. One dark evening, several followed her from her old cabin in the woods, hid in the brush, and watched her change into a cat and steal inside a home. She continued, as usual, placing a spell on the family. Then she jumped out the window in the form of the cat. She got to the barn and began to recite her spell to turn herself back into a woman. However, several people were waiting in the barn, and they jumped out in the middle of her magic. She could not transform completely from cat to woman, so she was left as half-woman, half-cat. She let out a bloodcurdling yowl and darted off into the darkness of night. But she is still around. Once in a while, she comes back, stealing a chicken or a lone child playing by itself in a yard.

Along King Shoals flowing toward Elk River where an old farmstead once stood and a Wampus Cat was born.

In some Appalachian folklore, the Wampus Cats in West Virginia were humans who came back from the dead in the form of a cat. Their return was to right some wrong against them. There is an old legend of the Wampus Cat of King Shoals with beginnings in what is now Wallback Wildlife Management Area.

In the early days, a couple moved to this fertile land between two creeks that ran into the Elk River—King Shoals Run and Upper King Shoals Run. They built a cabin on the Upper King, cleared the land to farm, and started a small family. Right away, they had two strapping boys who helped to work the prospering land. Many years would pass before the woman gave birth to another child—a baby girl. The family cherished the always-happy, sweet child, and the father was very fond of the infant and doted on her.

But when she was five or six months old, the little girl became quite sick with fever, and nothing they could do would make her well. Several days went by. The man told his wife that the fever would surely pass. It had when the boys would take sick, and the babe was strong and hardy. They should wait a couple more days before they called for help far away in Charleston. It was a long ride—the family was nearly thirty-six miles from the closest city with a doctor. And doctors were expensive. Two more days passed, and the child only got worse. She was wasting away. The husband finally gave way to his wife's pleas and saddled his old plow horse and took off, for he wanted his beloved daughter to live at all cost. It took some time to get to the city, then return with the doctor. By the time that the two arrived, the child had died. Heartbroken, the father buried his only daughter at the top of the hill between the two runs.

He buried her in a lone grave on the hill between the two runs.

The flat area where the farm stood.

He hardly spoke to anyone for many days and would spend his evenings sitting quietly on his porch grieving, telling himself it was his fault she died. He thought long and hard and wished he had gone for the doctor sooner. While he sat there a broken man, he listened to the splash of the water in the stream. He heard the sound of animals in this isolated pocket of the world—the roars of bears and hoots of owls. An occasional wolf would howl, and bobcats would scream.

One evening while he smoked his pipe in his rickety chair on the porch, he heard a caterwauling yowl of a wildcat he had never heard before. And it came from the direction where he had buried his cherished baby girl. He scoffed it off for a few days, then on the third night, he just knew something must be haunting that gravesite. And he made an oath to kill it.

The next night, the man took quiet strides to the little cemetery at dusk with his rifle. He waited in the cover of darkness and watched while the hours passed. However, no cry broke the still air. Defeated, he strolled back to his house and laid down in his bed. The yowl broke through the night sounds, a bloodcurdling cry sending shivers up the spines of those within the home. Tomorrow, he decided, he would return to the gravesite along with his dogs and after the sun had set entirely. He did return to the burial ground. It would be deep into the night when his dogs let out a ruckus of howls and barks. The man was dozing on pine needles. Something was nearby! He jumped up and followed the dogs' baying cries and found them barking into the canopy of a tree. He looked up, saw the dark outline of a huge cat, a mountain lion, perhaps about twenty to thirty feet above. He raised his gun, and the shot rang out, a booming echo rolling through the mountains as the beast crashed through the limbs and leaves and fell to the earth.

He stood there, staring at the ground where it fell. He was sure it was a mountain lion. Almost elated at his sure shot and skill, for the moment, his daughter's death was far from his mind. He had taken out his grief and anger at losing his child on this enormous mountain cat trespassing on his property.

King Shoals—and a Wampus Cat.

The man grabbed up a paw and dragged the heavy cat down to his barn, and hefted it up where he hung his pigs to bleed out. He left it to hang there, and he went back into his house. Sometime during that same night, the barn burned down. When they sifted through the ashes, there was no trace of the wildcat he caught.

It was baffling to his family, but not so to the man. For although he never heard the cry of the cat near the cemetery again, he knew something had gone wrong that night. He remembered the stories his grandparents passed down, of the dead seeking revenge in the form of a cat to correct an injustice. They called them Cattywampus or Wampus Cats.

He had been so caught up in his grief that he had not taken into consideration that the cat was his daughter in spirit form. He was the one who refused to get the doctor soon enough. It was his wrong that led her back from the grave. But she was too sweet a daughter to wreak out her vengeance. It was also he who shot her.

There have been increased sightings of panthers and panther-like creatures with glowing red eyes, long tails, and walking upright. Some report the beings to have the reek of a bucket full of mungy washcloths mixed with a skunk's odor. In 2007, a bow hunter said he saw a full-grown, male African lion weighing between 250 and 300 pounds in Big Roaring Creek at the base of Cold Knob Mountain on his private property in Greenbriar County. It paced around his homemade hunting shanty for nearly an hour.

There have been black panthers caught on trail cameras in Clay County and Wampus Cat sighting in Pleasants County. Could some be exotic releases? Or is it the Cherokee half-woman half-mountain lion, a witch, or a dead person arising from the grave? Perhaps we may never know—at least until we catch one in the flesh—or spirit. One thing is for sure—regardless if the animal is an exotic release or an actual Wampus Cat, both can cause some harm. As always, be wary and careful when exploring for the creatures!

Where can you look for the Wampus Cat?

Elk River King Shoals Public Access (*Across from Wallback*) *Elk River Rd, Clendenin, WV 25045 (38.504493, -81.231299)*

Parking for hiking Wallback: Elk River Road, Clendenin, WV 25045 (38.50582, -81.23277)
Where the Wampus Cat was found.

*The 11,758- acre **Wallback Wildlife Management Area** (Clay, Kanawha, Roane Counties) Co Route 13/17 and Elk River Road, Clendenin, WV 25045*
Remember to check for game hunting seasons in the areas you hike!

West Virginia

White Thing

White Thing of Morgan Ridge

Description: White with long, shaggy hair sometimes matted. Built like a dog, but as large as a bear. Some reports compare it to a lion-dog with a long white mane. Sabretooth fangs. Sharp claws. Appears and disappears ghost-like. Violent attacks that leave no scars/wounds afterward. Very fast and has been known to attack by biting and clawing. Runs on all fours. Walk on two legs. Attached to cemeteries.

Other Names: White Creature. Bear-Ape. Devil-Dog.

Location: Marion County, WV; Mingo County, WV

In the late 1800s, a young woman was riding her favorite mare home from a Saturday evening church meeting. Not two miles from her house, she was startled by a dreadful scream. Her horse bolted and danced about, panicking at something the young woman could not see. She could barely hold on to the reins while the horse reared, her forelegs held high off the ground. Just as the horse came down to all fours, the young woman saw it—The *White Thing*. It was nearly the horse's size with thick, white fur and razor-sharp teeth jutting outward from an elongated mouth.

The young woman kicked her mare's sides, urging her into a full gallop toward home. The White Thing burst from the woods onto the road and, with horrifying, high-pitched screams, pursued the rider side-by-side. Finally, near her home, the darkness consumed the beast. Still, filled with fear, she quickly dismounted at her family's barn and shooed the horse inside the building, deciding not to take the time to stall the animal. The next morning, the young woman and her father went out to search for the creature— tracks or fur or anything that would divulge what animal it could have been. As they reached the barn, though, they found the mare lying dead against the barn doors. Something had torn the hide from her flesh, and the mare had a horrified sneer to the lips.

Not all attacked by the white-coated beast with fang-like teeth and wrathful temperament left scars or death in their wake. Nearly 150 miles northeast of the previous region, Frank Kozul was a thirty-six-year-old miner at the Jordan NO 93 mine near Rivesville and Fairmont. He had a long walk home each night from work. Sometimes after eleven-hour shifts, he would take a shortcut across the ridges instead of taking the roundabout, longcut on the roads.

Morgan Ridge—where a man was chased down by a White Thing.

Well, he took that particular route for some time until one hot July night in 1929. When he started up the path on a shortcut along Morgan Ridge, he came face to face with something white and standing two feet above the ground. It had a strangely large head and a thick, bushy tail. It made no noise he could hear. Thinking he could scare it away, Frank kicked at the creature with the toe of his boot. His foot went right through. That is when the trouble began—the thing then started lunging at Frank. In his hand, he still had his lunch pail, so Frank wielded it like a sword, swinging at the White Thing. It did nothing but glide right through. He picked up a stick and began striking at the thing that was lunging at his arms and legs.

Frank knew he would have welts and scratches; he could feel them on his skin. Finally, after a battling chase, Frank passed a cemetery. It was here that the creature faded away. After returning home that evening and by the lantern light, Frank checked his arms and legs, but not a scratch marred his skin. He never again took a shortcut through the ridge.

Farmers from the same region near Rivesville had often related that a creature with a spine-tingling scream attacked their sheep, cows, and goats. When shot, the bullets would fly right through. More recently, in 1994, a man admitted to having witnessed, as a child, a white creature with thick shaggy hair and no discernable face floating next to his family's moving vehicle before it disappeared.

The White Thing is sometimes associated with Sheepsquatch, but White Thing is more often seen as having a mystical quality and does not have horns.

Where can you look for the White Thing?

Morgan Ridge Road Rivesville, WV 26588
(39.534067, -80.101782)

Morgan Ridge Road winds its way through isolated pockets of residences and woodland. It is near this area that Frank saw the White thing. You will have to take a drive-through, though. Most of the area is privately owned.

West
Virginia

Grafton Monster

Riverside Drive Monster

Description: 9-10 feet tall. Slick, seal-like sheen to the skin. No discernible head. Emits a whistling sound.

Other Names: Beast of Grafton. Riverside Drive Monster.

Location: Grafton, WV—Taylor County

The Grafton Monster was seen on Riverside Drive (right)—a headless creature with slick skin maybe still be roaming this area of the Tygart River.

Grafton has two of the United States Department of Veterans Affairs national cemeteries and was home to the first real Mothers' Day on May 12th, 1907. It is also known for one of West Virginia's biggest monster legends that started at 11:00 p.m. on June 16th of 1964.

A local reporter for the Grafton Sentinel, Robert Cockrell, witnessed the monster for the first time in his headlight beams as he rounded a curve at about fifty miles per hour on his way home from work on Riverside Drive.

He would describe it as: "a huge white obstruction on the right side of the road standing between the road and the riverbank on a cleared-off section of grass." Disconcerted, he continued his drive and went home. But within twenty minutes, his curiosity as a journalist eventually made him return with two friends to check out the area. The grass on the ground was matted, but there was no strange creature around. The trio checked the surrounding woods, the road, and along the riverbank. Still, they heard an eerie whistling coming from the riverbank. It appeared to follow them no matter what direction they turned to investigate. A June 18th edition of the Grafton Sentinel ran a short article written by Robert Cockrell about the sighting.

In just days, the streets were lined with cars bumper-to-bumper searching for the elusive beast described as nine to ten feet tall, having pale skin, and no discernible head. More than twenty people witnessed this creature along the river and at a nearby stone quarry, although local authorities played the event down as a great imagination or a hoax.

Where can you look for the Grafton Monster?

You can drive along Riverside Drive/Yates Avenue in Grafton, West Virginia, following the Tygart River as you go. Watch for the billboard marking the event placed along the route by Grafton native Brendan Gallagher, and maybe, just maybe, spy the monster for yourself—**Yates Avenue**, Grafton, West Virginia 26354 (39.3459, -80.0426)

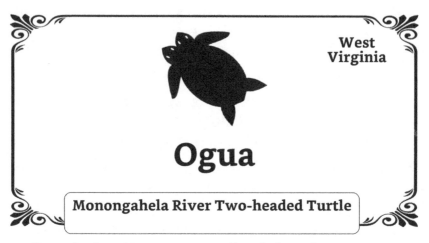

West Virginia

Ogua

Monongahela River Two-headed Turtle

Description: Monstrous two-headed turtle

Other Names: Monster Turtle.

Location: The   Monongahela   River—In   WV, Monongalia and Marion Counties

The Ogua is known to roam the Monongahela River.

The Ogua is a river monster that has been legendary since Native Indians roamed the waters around the Monongahela River. This creature looks like a monstrous two-headed turtle.

The Ogua works swiftly during the night, grabbing its prey and pulling its victim beneath the water to drown it before gobbling it up. Its prey are deer and occasional unwary people.

Where can you look for the Ogua?

The Caperton River Trail-*6-mile paved rail trail running through Morgantown. You can park at Hazel Ruby McQuain Park—185 Garrett Street, Morgantown, WV 26501 (39.629687, -79.959858)*

Mon River Trail S, *Round Bottom Road, Morgantown, WV 26508 (39.587336, -79.977970)*

West Virginia

Ohio River Monster

Giant Serpent on the Ohio River

Description: Ten feet long. Black in color. Eyes larger than those of a big dog.

Other Names: Giant Serpent.

Location: Near Parkersburg, WV—Wood County

In July of 1893, boaters in the Ohio River at Blennerhassett Island were stunned to discover a horrifying sea serpent moving around in the water and rounding their small skiff. Witnesses described the creature as ten feet long, black in color, and with eyes larger than those of a big dog. Thinking it was nothing more than a hoax, another party of boaters went out into the water and were surprised to see the same creature floating nearby.

Where can you look for the Ohio River Monster?

Blennerhassett Island Historical State Park: You can take a boat ride and watch for the creature, then walk the island to see if it comes into sight: 137 Juliana Street Parkersburg, WV 26101 (39.264914, -81.565030)

West Virginia

Cumberland Dragon

Acid-spitting Goosefoot

Description: Stands erect on two legs. Covered with black, brown, and light colored scales—in spots like rings. On the crown of its head which is large as a two-pound stone is a white tuft. It had huge, fiery red eyes.

Other Names: Goosefoot.

Location: Cumberland Mountains and Vicinity

The pull-off on US-19. If you stop at the scenic overlook off US-19 in Birch River, watch for the Cumberland Dragon.

The Cherokee-American Wars ran from 1776-1795 and involved a series of raids and battles between the Cherokee and settlers. Toward the end of the war, in February 1794, a detachment of American infantry infiltrated 15 miles into the Cumberland Mountains near Cove Creek in Tennessee.

Two men, one whose name was M'Donald, were sent in advance as spies. Working ahead, they came upon a creature only three steps from them that they had never seen before. It stood upright on two legs, was covered with black, brown, and golden scales in spots like rings. On the crown of its head, which was as large as a two-pound stone, there was a white tuft. It had huge, fiery-red eyes.

This strange oddity stood its ground even as M'Donald advanced toward it. Since he was given orders not to shoot anything but the enemy, he struck it with his sword. The creature jumped as high as eight feet in the air, then settled back to the spot it had taken off. It began to spew a red liquid like blood before it turned and ran into the thick brush. It left tracks that were similar to a goose. An article in the Pittsburgh Evening Gazette September 13th, 1794, related this after they reported on the creature: *The Indians report, that a creature inhabits that part of the mountain, of the above description, which, by its breath, will kill a man if he does not instantly immerse himself in water.* This creature can inhabit the woodland anywhere along the Cumberland Mountains, and you might see it driving near Powell Mountain. There is a great overlook. And while you are at it, watch for the ghost of Henry Young—a Confederate militiaman who was tragically shot on Powell Mountain. His spirit rides headless down this mountain road, Young's Monument Road.

Where can you look for the Cumberland Dragon?

Scenic overlook off US-19 in Birch River, West Virginia at Powell Mountain. US-19, Birch River, WV 26610
(38.463283, -80.782849)

You may also see this creature at: **Cove Creek Wildlife Management Area**. Jacksboro, TN 37757
(36.255992, -84.081946)

West
Virginia

Marrtown Banshee

Marrtown's Foretelling Screamer

Description: Appears as a withered older woman usually wearing rags. Wails and keens.

Other Names: Doppelganger.

Location: Marrtown, WV—Wood County

Along Marrtown Road where a Banshee foretold a death.

The Irish and the Scottish have passed down legends of a female spirit or fairy foretelling impending death by shrieking, wailing, or keening. The Irish call them *Bean Sidhe* and Scottish, *Bean Nighe*. At times, she is depicted as an old washer woman in raggedy clothing and gray cloak.

Other times, she has long and streaming white hair and dons a gray cloak over a green dress. She is usually quite tiny, between one and four feet tall!

When these ethnic groups settled in Ohio and West Virginia, they did not come alone. They also brought the fairies and lore of their ancestors. Such entered the Banshee into an area a little less than two miles from Parkersburg in a place called Marrtown. Legends say that the founder of this little town, Thomas Marr, was haunted by a Banshee. Several times while riding to work at the Baltimore and Ohio Railroad freight yard in 1874, sixty-one-year-old Marr was followed by a rider in a raggedy hood that would vanish from sight. He told his wife, Mary, this strange story, and little was thought of it until the evening a rider came to the back gate of the home. When Mary went out to welcome the guest, the horse and rider dressed in dark, ragtag clothing and hood disappeared into the night. It was February 6th, 1874. Thomas Marr was found dead at the freight depot only hours later. He had climbed to the top of the station box to clean out a stovepipe, fell, and broke his neck.

Family members related that the Banshee returned to wail when Mary died at age ninety. As she lay dead in her coffin, the sound of chains rang out in the attic, and a keening wail filled the air. Some believe the creature remains in this area. There have been reports of a woman wearing a ragged, black cape walking along WV-95 at Parkersburg near the W.H. Bickel Estate during stormy weather. Whether she forewarns people of impending death or is just a ghostly reminder of the past is unknown. But it is a fair warning if you feel a bit ill, avoid that area at all costs!

Where can you look for the Marrtown Banshee?

Along Marrtown Road, Parkersburg, WV 26101

(39.247505, -81.586930)

West Virginia

Giant Birds

Spruce Knob's Modern Roc

Description: Brown with white wings. Large beak. 15-foot wingspan. Attacks violently.

Other Names: Modern Roc. Thunderbird. Giant Eagle.

Location: Webster County, Pendleton County, WV

Spruce Knob.

On a Friday in early March of 1895, ten-year-old Landy Junkins, living in an isolated pocket near Bergoo, was sent by her mother to Joe Warnick's cabin to check on his ill wife.

It was only a mile and a half away, and Landy set off just after noon. It was only about a half-hour trek one-way. But when Landy had not returned by four or five o'clock, Missus Junkins grew uneasy and sent the girl's father along the same route to find the girl. The father set off, sure his daughter was at the Warnick's helping the family. However, when he reached the Warnick's home, he found the young girl had never arrived.

Lonely stretch of water in Webster County near Bergoo and Webster Springs.

Quickly, neighbors formed a search party. There was still snow on the ground, so they could track Landy's steps to a point just a half-mile from the Warnick's to a field where a farmer had harvested buckwheat the previous fall. Then, the small footprints left the path as if the young girl had, in a panic, suddenly bolted. They paused about twenty feet away, where her tracks merged as if she had spun in a circle trying to avoid something. Beyond, any traces of the girl vanished.

The search continued through the fields and woods, night and day, but those who looked for Landy came up empty-handed. No one found the young girl. Circumstances occurring over the next week would explain the puzzling disappearance of young Landy. A farmer named Hance Hardrick, ten miles from Bergoo, kept his sheep stalled in a bark-covered outbuilding. After returning from town, he noticed a sheep missing. Upon further inspection, he saw a hole in the ceiling. There were no tracks around the building. The conclusion was that something huge had descended from the sky and snatched up a full-grown sheep.

Peter Swadley, a local hunter, was pursuing a bear on Piney Ridge near Addison (Webster Springs) with his dog, Gunner. He came upon a tiny clearing and heard an awful scream louder than a panther. In a matter of breaths, a huge bird swooped down on him, digging its monstrous talons through his thick coat and into his flesh. Stunned, Swadley dropped his rifle and could not reach his knife. With only the use of his hands, Swadley beat off his attacker, but not without a terrible fight. The giant bird ripped his arms and legs with talons and beak and nearly tore his scalp clean from his head. The dog had run ahead before the attack, but Swadley's cries brought him back to the man. Suddenly, his dog cut through the woods and lunged forward into the meadow and at the bird. Swadley took a moment to free himself and was barely able to crawl away to safety while he watched his dog become the new target of the bird. Instantly, the bird gutted the dog and carried it away in its talons. A neighbor later rescued Swadley.

Rube Nihiser, a deputy sheriff in the county, was out hunting with his son on Sugar Run while light snow fell. They followed a deer trail through hemlocks and to a clearing where both stopped stunned. Ahead, there was a doe and fawn huddling while a huge bird circled just above.

The bird swooped down, attacking the deer with giant talons and a thick beak. Nihiser raised his rifle and shot at the bird as it plucked the bleating fawn from the doe's side.

The father and son retreated home after firing a couple of blind shots into the air and hopefully scaring the giant bird away. The two men would describe the bird as a deep brown with eyes wider than an owl's eyes and a wingspan of fifteen feet, and with white on the wings and light underneath. The body was as large as a man's, and the cry, ear-splitting. It took off toward the area of Spruce Knob in Pendleton County, where the rocks atop the enormous mountain appear like snaggleteeth. Many believed that it was on this high peak where few would climb that the bird nested and called its home.

But Webster County was not the only area known for giant eagle-like birds. In mid-May of 1907, D.M. Riffee and his two sons were in a field near Clarksburg (Harrison County), West Virginia. One of the boys, an eight-year-old, had walked a little farther away when a huge bird swooped down and tried to pick him up. The boy lurched to one side, and the bird missed. Quickly the father came forward, and the monstrous beast flew away.

Where can you look for the Giant Birds?

Spruce Knob –(the highest point in West Virginia) was believed to be the nesting place of these huge birds—Spruce Knob, Spruce Knob Trail and platform, Riverton, WV 26814 (38.699868, -79.532865)

Spruce Knob and Spruce Knob Observation Tower–*Is just a short, easy hike from the parking lot. Whispering Spruce Trail (a half mile) circles the knob and provides panoramic views.*
It is only about 21 miles from Seneca Rocks. Spruce Knob, Spruce Knob Trail and tower, Riverton, WV 26814
(38.699868, -79.532865)
While you are visiting, keep a lookout for Bigfoot who have been sighted here. Footprints have been found at the base of the mountain and knocking heard.

Seneca Rocks National Recreation Area is in Monongahela National Forest and offers the perfect habitat for these birds You can get an excellent view for Giant Birds at the overlook platform: Trail: 1.3 miles (2.6 miles round-trip) Seneca Rocks Trailhead—WV-28 N/WV-55 E, Seneca Rocks, WV 26884 (38.835717, -79.372418) Trail has steps and steep climb.

West
Virginia

Grant Town Goon

Coal Mine Dump Goon

Description: Bigfoot-like.

Other Names: Bigfoot. Goon.

Location: Found in the coal mining dumps and waste areas around Grant Town—Marion County, WV

Grant Town was formed along the Paw Paw Creek in 1901 with the opening of the Federal Coal and Coke Company. It prospered, and Federal No. 1 remained open for 84 years. It closed in 1985. But it was in the 1970s when a hairy Bigfoot-like creature stalked the waste areas around the old coal mine near abandoned mine shafts. The Grant Town Power Plant is now located in the region of the old mine.   **Where can you find the Grant Town Goon?**

Chink Run Road in Grantsville (39.563666, -80.166169) runs along the land abutting the old Federal Coal and Coke Company property. Be wary of private property outside the bounds of the roadway proper.

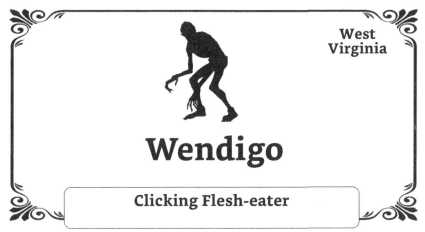

West
Virginia

Wendigo

Clicking Flesh-eater

Description: Pale and pasty gray flesh hanging on bones. Tall—5-7 feet. Lanky with long arms and legs.

Other Names: Windigo. Weedigo. Witiku.

Location: Poverty-stricken areas. Areas where the homeless hang out and missing people are not noticed.

If a Wendigo walked Crown City Wildlife Area.

The Wendigo appears as an emaciated creature and somewhat human-like—a gaunt corpse of not more than flesh and bones, tall and skinny with long arms and legs.

Among the Algonquian, there were several forms of Wendigo acknowledged:

-Man-eating skeletal giants who lurk in the woods and hide in caves.

-Humans who dreamed of ice spirits and became possessed by the Wendigo spirit craved human flesh in times of starvation and disease. An evil spirit would possess the starving, sick, and weak and give them an unquenchable desire to eat human flesh. Their hearts are said to turn to ice.

-Humans who resort to cannibalism to survive were not uncommon in isolated pockets of the United States in its early years when snow and ice, flooding, and disease cut off people from their food sources.

If it cannot feed, the skin gets tighter, the beast skinnier. The creature makes a bellowing or roaring sound and clucks and whistles softly through lips that are decaying. More common to the upper Great Lakes region and Eastern woodlands, it has followed the path of those Powhatan, Cree, and Ojibway and settlers who made their way into West Virginia's forests. Elusive, the creature is tough to find, although there is a way to know if it is nearby. An old story offers up a way to tell if the Wendigo is around—

A widow of Native Indian blood lived on an old mountain road. She took ill, and visitors began to call to check on her. Each person who came heard a peculiar *click-click-click* while they were there. Neighbors searched the home to find this unusual sound, but no one could locate the source. At first, they believed it was just crickets or other house pests. Then a woman who had paid a visit stepped outside to leave. The *click-click-click* followed her along the stone walkway to the little picket fence at the edge of the property. It did not stop until she had passed through the gate.

Another man heard the *click-click-click* on his way home as if someone snapping their fingernails together was walking close behind. When he reached his front door, it stopped. His wife listened to the sound, too, as she met him there. Not one person could track the sound to any one location, and it went from room to room of the old widow's home, inside and outside through her garden and sheds.

Finally, two young men boasted they would not stop until they uncovered the identity of the *click-click-click*. They started at the front door where it began— *click-click-click*. It stopped. Then they raced out into the garden where it began again—*click-click-click*. Around and around the inside and the outside of the house, they went, chasing the sound. Over fields and rocks and creeks and hills, they followed the noise until they finally stopped in exasperation. *Click-click-click*. Beaten, they tucked their chins and went back to the house and told the old woman of their trial. She listened to their story, then held up a finger in the air and told them— "That's a Wendigo. Do not try to see it or find it. You cannot. A Wendigo (Indian spirit) will never show itself." After a bit of time, the woman died, and no one heard the *click-click-click* anymore.

A well-known shaman of the Cree claimed to have killed over fourteen Wendigos during his lifetime to protect his people. Some were sent to him by enemies; others were family members who became possessed with the desire to eat human flesh during famines. He was eventually arrested at age eighty-seven for these killings but was acquitted.

Not all of us have this protection from the Wendigo. Be wary in the woods, dark city streets, and around old mining shafts and recess caves. These are a few of the places people have found them. Listen for the *click-click-click* and give yourself some time to run.

Where can you look for the Wendigo?

There are a few stray reports of Wendigos near **Huntington**, and the closest area to watch and listen for them would be the remoter areas of Crown City Wildlife Area (38.640718, -82.327401). But I think it is more often that *they* come for you than *you* go to find them!

The Wendigo can take on the form of a dark creature with horns of a stag. It has the scent of a decomposing corpse. It may look weak and emaciated, but don't be fooled. The Wendigo craves flesh and is as blood-thirsty as any starving beast. It will hunt you down and eat you. Just listen while you walk in the woods or dark places for the signature click-click-click like fingernails daintily tapping on wood. And if you hear it, run!

West Virginia

Vegetable Man

Bloodsucking Alien

Description: At least 6-7 feet tall. Green skeletal stalk-like frame and yellow, sickly eyes. Long fingers with suction cups and needle tips.

Other Names: Veggie Man.

Location: Fairmont, WV

A remote area outside Fairmont. While hunting near Fairmont and Rivesville, a man had a strange encounter.

Jennings Frederick was around nineteen-years-old when he went out to bow hunt for woodchuck one hot July day of 1968 near Fairmont. Without much luck, he was about to call it a day when he heard a strange high-pitched jabbering.

It seemed to become more frantic until, within his mind, he heard the words— "You need not fear me. I wish to communicate. I come as friends. We know of you all . . .I wish for medical assistance. I need your help."

Dumbfounded, Frederick absently reached into his pocket to get his handkerchief tucked within and felt something tangling around his hand like a vine of thorns. He quickly snapped his hand out and stared down at a strange, green hand that was clasped to his. If that was not odd enough, the fingers had suction cups with needle-like tips. The grip tightened until Frederick felt a pang like a needle was inserted into his flesh. He knew the creature was taking blood from him as its eyes changed from pale to a bloodshot red. But Frederick was mesmerized by the voice and the whirling of the red in the eyes. He felt numbed and unable to move for nearly a minute before the vegetable creature released him, turned, and walked back into the woods. He was certain he heard some sort of engine-like sound as if it was an alien aircraft.

His hand had throbbed then, and Frederick could see a small pockmark on the skin where the needle-like fingertip had jabbed his flesh. He knew his story was too incredible for anyone to believe, so he later told family members it was a cut from a thorn or brier. Frederick would not admit to the encounter until some time later when he divulged it to famous writer and paranormal investigator Gray Barker. Frederick described this strange creature as taller than himself with a green skeletal stalk-like frame and yellow, sickly eyes. The fingers were seven inches long. He believed it was alien. Frederick's account has been the only known encounter with the creature that has come to be known as Vegetable Man.

Where can you find Vegetable Man?
Outlying areas of Fairmont and Rivesville, West Virginia.

West
Virginia

The Bigfoot

Sasquatch. Bigfoot. Ya-hoo. Wild Man. Skunk Ape. Grassman—what about all those names?

Sasquatch- The English adaptation of the Salish (North American Indian tribe of the Pacific Northwest) word: *Sasq'ets*, which means "wild man." The Salish believed the upright-walking, hairy wild men seen in their remote pocket of the world could move between the physical and spiritual realm. The name was coined in the late 1920s by J.W. Burns, a government Indian agent/teacher, who believed in their existence. The term Sasquatch is used more in the Pacific Northwest. By the way, Skamania County, Washington, considers itself a Sasquatch refuge, and authorities regard the creature as an endangered species. They adopted an ordinance protecting the Sasquatch—oh, and the innocent people out in the woods possibly mistaken for the Sasquatch. The law, in part, states:

"Whereas, both legend and purported recent sightings and spoor support this possibility, and Whereas, this creature is generally and commonly known as a "Sasquatch", "Yeti", "Bigfoot", or "Giant Hairy Ape", all of which terms may hereafter be used interchangeably, and Whereas, publicity attendant upon such real or imagined sightings as resulted in an influx of scientific investigators as well as casual hunters, most of which are armed with lethal weapons . . .therefore be It resolved that any premeditated, willful, and wanton slaying of any such creature shall be deemed a felony punishable by a fine not to exceed Ten Thousand Dollars ($10,000) and/or imprisonment in the county jail—

Picture of Gerald Crew holding cast. Used with permission of the Times Standard and Media News Group: Huge Footprint Found on Road— Oct 6th, 1958

Bigfoot – Gerald Crew made "Bigfoot" a household name. Crew was a cat skinner for the Granite Logging Company and the Wallace Brothers Logging Company in the 1950s. He was the one who bulldozed the brush and stumps left over after the logging crews cleared an area. One day while working in an area of Bluff Creek in California and getting ready to climb onto his bulldozer, Gerald saw a huge footprint in the mud. He believed he was the victim of a practical joke by the loggers until finding more tracks on the construction site. On October 5th, 1958, he presented a plaster cast of one footprint from Bluff Creek Valley to The Humboldt Times. They printed his story—*16 Foot Footprint Has Natives in Dither*. The title would have "Bigfoot" beneath it. The name would stick.

The famous Frame 352 from the video reel where Roger Patterson and Bob Gimlin had their encounter with the Sasquatch on the banks of Bluff Creek around 1:30 p.m. on Friday, October 20th, 1967. If you are in California, you can visit Bluff Creek near the site. Bigfoot Scenic Byway Orleans, CA 95556 (41.241476, -123.654634) Six Rivers National Forest

Bigfoot, Sasquatch, Ya-hoo—they go by many names in many regions of the U.S., but there are a few characteristics that seem to remain about the same in eyewitness sightings—

They range from seven to ten feet tall, are hairy, and walk upright. They have broad shoulders. The face is flat, and the ears are on the side of the head. The arms and legs are long, and the fur may range in various colors, including black, brown, blonde, or white.

They are all similar types of what experts have termed "Relict Hominoids" (leftover or survivor from the same kind of primates, including humans, our ancestors, and anthropoid apes). Dr. Russell Jones, who wrote *Tracking the Stone Man: West Virginia's Bigfoot*, has collected information over the years suggesting that regardless of the general color of the hair seen by witnesses, that under a microscope, there is a slight reddish tint to the strands. He also states: "Bigfoot hair covers most of the body except the palms of the hands, soles of the feet, and some of the face. It is an omnivore, eating both plants and animals."

With that in mind, I have given locations where witnesses have sighted these Relict Hominoids. I have also noted any special features observed and the local nicknames bestowed besides Sasquatch or Bigfoot in the region sighted.

For more information on Bigfoot:

-Tracking the Stone Man: West Virginia's Bigfoot. Dr. Russell Jones

-Bigfoot Field Researchers Organization (BFRO) bfro.net/

-Sasquatch Field Guide Identifying, Tracking and Sighting North America's Relict Hominoid by Dr. Jeff Meldrum

-WV *C.A.S.E*—Les O'Dell—WV Cryptids and Strange Encounters

West
Virginia

Bigfoot-*Wild Man*

Flatwoods
Sutton

Description: Reddish-brown. Cone-shaped head. No visible neck. 7 feet tall. Cross between man and monkey.

Names: Hairy Man. Wild Man. Bigfoot. Squatch.

Location: Flatwoods/Sutton—Braxton County, WV

In March of 1919, Luther Douglas was returning from a lodge meeting near Flatwoods, West Virginia. He passed the barn of a local farmer Ed Wiley and heard a noise. Not thinking the sound was anything unusual and was most likely a dog, Douglas continued onward and started to pass a vacant house just a short distance away. He heard the loud slam of a door and then watched in disbelief as a wild-looking man dressed in rags with long hair and a beard ran out of the vacant house door. In his hand, this wild man was brandishing a knotted club and uttering indecipherable and horrifying sounds. Fearing for his life and knowing that there had been a rash of chicken and piglet thefts from local farms, Douglas whipped out his pistol and fired two shots at the wild man. Immediately the beast turned and fled.

A hundred years have passed, and people have begun to speak out about seeing the wild man near Flatwoods again. There have been a varied number of reports of a Bigfoot-like creature at Sutton Lake just outside the town of Flatwoods.

A story comes from Les O'Dell, who runs West Virginia Cryptids and Strange Encounters (WV CASE)—an online portal for those who have encountered cryptids and strange creatures to share their accounts. At Sutton Dam, a fisherman was startled one day by a seven-foot-tall hairy man-like creature moving swiftly up a sharp incline before disappearing into the woods.

About eight to ten miles away outside Frametown, a WV CASE follower had a bigfoot sighting during daylight hours in August of 1987. On a camping trip, the family had just finished eating breakfast at a remote encampment. They looked up toward the riverbank and sat stunned while an eight-foot "squatch" walked right through the camp, heading toward the bottom of the mountain where there was a gas line clearing. It slipped into the woods. The woman described the bigfoot—"It was reddish-brown with a cone-shaped head, no neck, and about four feet wide." The next year, hikers found rocks larger than a car hood standing on end in a creek bed along an isolated section.

Where can you look for the Wild Man of Flatwoods?

Sutton Dam —*County Route 17/1 Sutton, WV 26601 (38.660118, -80.690924)*

Old tracks near Centralia
(38.612408, -80.564005)
Hiking: Elk River Wildlife Management Area—*1628 Bakers Run Road, Sutton, WV 26601 (38.635875, -80.576779)*
Camping/Trails available from US Army Corp.

West Virginia

Bigfoot-*Ya-hoo*

Monongahela National Forest
Camden on the Gauley
Richwood

Description: 6 feet tall. Red-brown hair. Bear-like.

Names: Bigfoot. Ya-hoo.

Location: Monongahela National Forest and Cranberry Wildlife Management Area—Nicholas, Webster, Pocahontas and Greenbrier Counties, WV

In the Cranberry Wildlife Management Area (Richwood, WV), while hunting squirrel, a young man came across a hairy creature about six to seven-feet tall watching him from behind a tree. In 2007, about midnight, a driver worked his way along Cranberry Ridge Road and through the Monongahela National Forest Cranberry Wildlife Management Area. He was taking a shortcut, heading towards the town of Camden-on-Gauley and eventually home.

He made a turn on County Route 7/6, passing a small camping area, and continued on his way. Suddenly, about four miles from town, something lurched across the road by the car. It was large and hairy, and the driver's first thought was that it was someone walking around in a monkey suit. It was approximately six feet tall, walked upright, and was covered in reddish-brown hair. Impulsively, he hit his horn.

It tore through the brush at breakneck speed and disappeared into the darkness. The realization rushed through the man—it was not someone in a monkey suit at all. He had seen Bigfoot.

After relating the strange adventure to his grandmother, she told the young man his story was not that incredible at all. The area he had been driving was known for many years for these strange creatures the locals had dubbed *Ya-hoos* for the eerie sound of the calls. They even had a nickname for the area—*Ya-hoo Holler*.

Where can you look for the Ya-hoo?

*Spotting area near **Ya-hoo Holler**—the perfect place for large creatures to live—surrounded by Cranberry Wilderness, a mix of 750 acres of bogs (Cranberry Glades Botanical Area) and deep forests. The graveled and rugged Co Route 7/6 (Cranberry Ridge Road) from Camden-On-Gauley to Richwood (This is the edge of the **Monongahela National Forest** where private property and national forest mingle. So please be wary of private property). A drive from Co Route 48: (38.362869, -80.589068) along Co Route 7/6 to the Cranberry River (38.295605, -80.526496) This is rugged road. Also Cranberry Glades hiking trails: (38.185451, -80.281178)*

This is the place I had my own experience. I was taking a pic from my jeep window and heard 2 knocks. I figured it was somebody hammering. Why? I do not know. It is in the middle of nowhere. I started to open my door and something HUGE jumped into the thick, thick brush out of sight. There were 2 more knocks like a warning that I was there. Then this horrible, ghastly stench of boiled cabbage and skunk spray filled the air so badly, it lingered in my jeep for a twenty-long-minute-ride.

Cranberry Wilderness trails in the Monongahela National Forest -
*A backwoods hike deep into the wilderness that's another perfect
secluded habitat for bears and Bigfoot—*
*—One Parking Access- Kennison Mountain Trail Hillsboro, WV
24946 (38.186001, -80.281047) As you drive the roads around
the forest, you'll see many pull-offs and hiking trails.*

Cranberry Tri-Rivers Rail Trail- *Parking Access
along the Cherry River: Cranberry Tri-Rivers Rail
Trail Richwood, WV 26261
(38.256823, -80.601133)*

West Virginia

Bigfoot-*Apple Devil*

Marlinton

Description: 4-5 feet tall. Large and hairy creature walking on two feet. Pointy fangs. Has a sour, musty scent.

Names: Apple Devil. Apple Picker.

Location: Marlinton, WV— Pocahontas County, WV

One area near Marlinton had an upswing of Bigfoot-type hominoids in the 1960s. The creature was described as hairy and could run at high speeds. They called them Apple Devils or Apple Pickers because the creatures seemed to prefer the apples in their orchards. Farmers reported branches broken on their apple trees and the fruit stripped from the limbs along with broken fences. It left a rank odor.

Where can you look for the Apple Devils?

The **Greenbrier River Trail** is a 78-mile rail-trail cutting through the remotest regions of West Virginia. It has tunnels and bridges—and goes through **Marlinton**. There are many trailheads and maps available online.

The closest parking to town—
In Marlinton: Greenbrier River Trail Parking:
9th St, Marlinton, WV 24954
(38.221694, -80.094338)

Watoga State Park—Start of Jesse's Cove Trail

Watoga State Park—
Jesse's Cove Trailhead-
At Riverside Campground by Site 6 (38.110505, -80.176127)
T.M. Cheek Memorial Overlook-
Forest Route 821 (38.110909, -80.119618)
Ann Bailey Trail-
Park and Forest Route 821 (38.106562, -80.127029)

Apple Devils are only 3-4 feet high.

West
Virginia

Bigfoot-*Canyon Monster*

Blackwater Falls State Park

Description: Bipedal. Dark fur—black or brown.

Names: Canyon Monster.

Location: Blackwater Falls State Park—Tucker County, WV

There are overlooks at Blackwater Falls State Park—At the Lodge: 1584 Blackwater Lodge Road, Davis, WV 26260 (39.108342, -79.496952) They can be crowded, but you can get an overall view.

Blackwater Falls State Park where many sightings of the Canyon Monster have occurred. It shouldn't be surprising. Just a few steps off the park map, you can disappear in dense and rough terrain with thick brush and a mixture of spruce, hemlocks, birch and maples. There are meadows where voles, mice, squirrels and rabbits roam. There are streams with fish. It is the perfect mixture of habitat for both meat-eaters and vegetation-eaters. And things that don't want to be found!

Blackwater Falls State Park is named for the Blackwater River waterfalls rushing through an eight-mile gorge—Blackwater Canyon. The black water flowing through the valley got its amber color from the tannic acids of the fallen hemlock and spruce needles. It runs from Davis to the confluence of the Blackwater River. It is here eyewitnesses have reported the Bigfoot dubbed *Canyon Monster*.

Blackwater Falls State Park—Canaan Loop Road—It is more like a trail than a 4-wheel-drive-only road after the Lindy Point outlook. Figuring we were not going to find any Bigfoot through the windshield anyway, we got out and hiked. It is beautiful. Canaan Loop Road is where a Bigfoot footprint had been found.

In 1960, a group of campers were in a remote woodland near the town of Davis. As one young man was gathering firewood, he felt a sharp poke at his ribs. Believing it was one of his friends pestering him, he turned and found himself staring face to face with what he could only describe as a *horrible monster*. The campers all saw the creature as it darted off into the forest. The man described the creature as "—having two huge eyes that shone like big balls of fire. It stood every bit of eight feet tall and had long shaggy hair all over its body, and its eyes were very far apart."

Terrified, the campers chose to stay instead of leaving in the dark. The next morning, they discovered huge footprints on the trail that the monster had left running to the woods.

Blackwater Falls State Park—Lindy Point Overlook—A great place to get a full view of the canyon and perhaps spy the monster. We found both bear tracks and bear scat (poop) along the trail.

There were three sightings of bear the day before. Bear and Bigfoot seem to like the same habitat, so this might be a great place to check out.
Lindy Point Trail Head—Canaan Loop Road, Thomas, WV 26292 (39.100115, -79.525178)

In 2007, a footprint was found in an overgrown area about fifty-yards from Canaan Loop Road near Blackwater Falls State Park. Others have had encounters with Bigfoot in the area—a couple driving outside nearby Davis were rambling along when something huge, about seven feet tall, jumped from a rock wall, stopped in the path of their van, and stared into the windshield. Just after, five similar creatures, but smaller—only three to four feet tall, followed across the same path before disappearing into the brush while screaming and screeching to each other.

The driver got out of the vehicle where the creature had crossed the path, staring into the brush only to find the smaller ones peering curiously back at him from behind a tree. It would not be the only meeting this family would have with these Bigfoot. Throughout the years, when visiting, they have heard the same screaming coming from the area between the towns of Davis and Thomas.

Where else can you look for the Canyon Monster?

Blackwater Canyon Trail – *The Blackwater Canyon Trail runs from Thomas to Hendricks (through Blackwater Falls), a rugged 10.5-mile one-way hike/bike—the old train tracks run through the Monongahela National Forest and were once (1880s) used to haul coal and lumber. You can hike/mountain bike the entire trail or just a bit of it. Trailhead Parking in Thomas: 250 State Hwy 32, Thomas, WV 26292 (39.150708, -79.497912)*

West
Virginia

Bigfoot

Canaan Valley National Wildlife Refuge—Camp 70

Description: Bipedal, primate-like creature. At least 250 pounds. A mixture of shaggy and flowing black hair with white-gray highlights. Somewhat pointy ears.

Names: Bigfoot. Sasquatch.

Location: Canaan Valley National Wildlife Refuge— Tucker County, WV

Canaan Valley National Wildlife Refuge Camp 70 Parking Area
Camp 70 Road, Davis, WV 26260 (39.135661, -79.405250)

In 2009, a hunter parked in the Camp 70 parking lot at Canaan Valley National Wildlife Refuge about four miles from Davis, West Virginia. It was 3:00 in the afternoon, a little later than he liked to start on a hunt. It would be dark soon. He made a hasty hike up an old logging road behind the parking area and began to scout for deer. After a while, he worked his way down into a valley via a secondary ice-frozen road. Unable to hike his way along the road without the sound of ice crunching beneath his boots, the hunter worked himself into a copse of trees and settled in to hunt.

It was not long before he heard the crackling of brush breaking—a sure sign deer were coming into a grassy area to feed. Feeling secure that he could get nearer to the sounds, he moved closer and scoped the trees with his rifle. But what he saw were not deer at all. He was stunned—his eyes homed in on a vague silhouette, then cleared to what he was sure was a bipedal, primate-like creature. It appeared to weigh at least two-hundred-and-fifty pounds, had a mixture of shaggy and flowing black hair with white-gray highlights, and bore somewhat pointy ears. The creature was staring at him and moved from a sitting position to a standing position. It then walked the expanse of the river basin and exited into the trees. The hunter did not pursue. The light was fading, and a slight feeling of unease sent him immediately heading toward his vehicle.

Where can you look for Bigfoot nearby?

Canaan Valley National Wildlife Refuge: Camp 70 Trails—Trails travel through meadows, forest, wetlands. Camp 70 Road, Davis, WV 26260 (39.135678, -79.405270)

West
Virginia

Bigfoot

New River Gorge

Description: 7 feet tall. Brownish-blonde fur. Wide, owl-like eyes. Face like a troll doll's face. Long, thick fingers. Dark fingernails.

Names: Bigfoot.

Location: New River Gorge—Fayette County, WV

New River Gorge where Bigfoot are seen.

In the autumn of 2007, an experienced deer hunter was hiking in the New River Gorge. The evening was setting in.

He noted he would only have a couple of hours left before packing up. Some movement in the brush caught his attention, and he raised his gun, eyeing something brown in the scope. It was a head, but it was certainly not a deer! He blinked with surprise—it was something he knew was not a deer or a bear—this creature he saw had two huge eyes, and both were fixed on him. That is until it simply vanished. So shocked by the animal, the hunter was less than happy that he had to go the same direction the creature disappeared to get to his vehicle!

The witness would later tell Bigfoot Field Researchers Organization Investigator, Russ Jones, the following: "It was very cool looking—about seven feet tall, it had very dark large pupils, and around the pupils, its eyes were almost owl -like—it had brownish blonde fur, and it had a visible face— it almost looked like the troll faces that you used to put on your pencils as kids— Really—but, it was very clean looking and not what you would expect—its fingers were long and thick with no fur, and it had dark fingernails."

The New River Gorge from Hawk's Nest Overlook —49 Co Route 60/23, Ansted, WV 25812 (38.122999, -81.127447)

Hikers along the many trails and campers staying in the New River Gorge have long reported finding tracks that do not belong to a bear or a barefooted man with a size 37AA foot and smelling the deep odor many link to the scent of Bigfoot. The area has many abandoned ghost towns, habitat filled with prey animals, fruits and berries, and acre upon acre of isolated forests.

Where can you look for Bigfoot along New River?

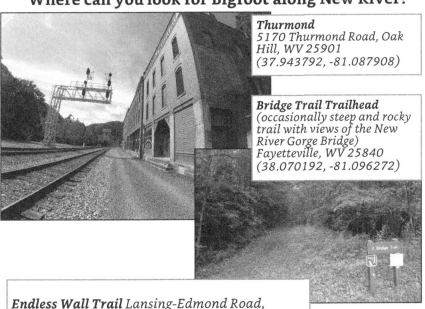

Thurmond
5170 Thurmond Road, Oak Hill, WV 25901
(37.943792, -81.087908)

Bridge Trail Trailhead
(occasionally steep and rocky trail with views of the New River Gorge Bridge)
Fayetteville, WV 25840
(38.070192, -81.096272)

Endless Wall Trail Lansing-Edmond Road, Edmond, WV 25837 (38.063157, -81.056670)

And if you like remote and the adventure of exploring a coal mining ghost town, Nuttalburg offers both—the perfect habitat for Bigfoot with recess caves and isolation and an old ghost town to check out.

Nuttalburg:
Keeneys Creek Road
New Haven, WV 25840
(38.050100, -81.039921)

West
Virginia

Bigfoot

Webster County– *Hairy One*

Description: 6 feet tall. Stands erect. Bigfoot-like.

Other Names: The Hairy One. Braxton Beast.

Location: Hickory Flats, WV—Webster County

Backroads near Hickory Flats.

Shortly before 11:00 p.m. on Friday, December 30th, 1960, twenty-five-year-old Charles Stover was driving his Dutch Oven Bakeries delivery truck on a lonely backroad near Hickory Flats. He rounded a curve, and before him was what he described as a six-foot "—monster standing erect, with hair all over his face and body."

He almost hit it but stopped his truck a short distance away. The monster stood there looking at him, then roared and went away. Shaken, he rushed to the closest filling station/restaurant and went inside to calm down with a cup of coffee, which he said he could hardly drink because his hands were shaking so badly. He told his chilling story to some men at the restaurant, and they quickly formed a posse, arming themselves with rifles. They followed Stover back to the spot. Nothing remained but overturned stones on the icy roadway. Days later, they found that others reported cries in the woods in the same area.

Where can you look for Bigfoot in Webster County?

Take a drive along Hickory Flats County Route 9/1
Erbacon, WV 26203 (38.520919, -80.633012)

West Virginia

Bigfoot-*Yellow Gape*

Monongahela National Forest

Description: 8 feet tall. Hair stands on end when provoked. Yellow eyes glow. Rotten sulfur-like scent.

Other Names: Yellow Gape. Bigfoot.

Location: Monongahela National Forest—Pocahontas County, WV

Williams River Road—where the Yellow Gape has made an appearance.

In October of 1961, W.C. Priestley was working his way to a hunting site for turkey season. He was following Gene Williams Forest and Mont Priestley driving a camper bus.

Up until that point, W.C. Priestley's vehicle had been running just fine. Suddenly, it began to sputter before completely stopping. "Then," Priestley said. "I saw it. To my left, beside the road, stood this monster with long hair pointing straight up toward the sky. I was so scared I could not move. I do not know how long I sat there until the boys missed me and backed the bus back to where I was. It seemed the monster was very much afraid of the bus and dropped his hair, and to my surprise, as soon as he did this, my car started to run again."

Priestley did not say anything to his buddies. He turned the key, and the car started as if nothing had happened at all. Then just as the camper bus started off again, Priestley's car sputtered like it was shorting out. Sure enough, the hairy monster was by the road again. The second time the bus backed up, the monster disappeared. Undaunted, Priestley admitted he did not tell Gene Williams Forest and Mont Priestley about seeing the hairy monster. He was more afraid they would not go deer hunting when it arrived in the upcoming months! **Where can you look for the Yellow Gape in this section of the Monongahela National Forest?**

There are pull-offs along Williams Road. A mile up is the three forks of Williams River, Monongahela National Forest-Edray, WV (Three Forks Area - Webster Springs, WV 26288
(38.3403908, -80.3761906)

West
Virginia

Bigfoot-*Polk Gap Monster*
Poke Holler Monster

Polk Gap and Poke Hollow at Twin Falls

Description: 7-10 feet tall. Light. Bigfoot-like.

Other Names: Polk Holler Monster.

Location: Polk Gap, and Poke Hollow at Twin Falls, Saulsville, Maben, WV—Wyoming County

The old Polk Gap Road before it ends in private property around the gap.

It walks upright with broad shoulders and long arms and legs. It looks like a cross between man and ape. Whatever it is, folks have been seeing a Bigfoot-like creature near Twin Falls State Park, Saulsville, and Maben for years.

It appears to come from deep in the woods around a place called Polk Gap (such, Polk Gap Monster) and the road that dead-ends into it, and also just down the same road after it crosses over WV-97 in Poke Hollow off Poke Hollow Road (Poke Holler Monster), a dark hollow that is now inside Twin Falls State Park.

Polk Gap Road is almost hidden just off WV-97. It is gravel and dirt and meanders to a bitter end at a hunting club roadblocked by gates and posted NO TRESPASSING signs. A little farther is the gap—Polk Gap—where the road and the monster got one of its names. Its range extends three and a half miles from the gap—crossing WV-97 and to Poke Hollow Road until it gets to Poke Hollow at Twin Falls State Park. I have had several folks quietly reveal their moms and dads, grandmas and grandpas passed down they heard it screaming in those woods and saw the monster dodging them in the trees before the golf course was there and the State of West Virginia built the beautiful lodge.

Poke Holler—where a Bigfoot-like monster once lived (and maybe still does). There is a trail running beside it at Twin Falls State Park.

The quiet neighborhood near the Oceana Town Hall in Oceana where the monster was seen—surrounded by deep forest on all sides—it doesn't seem so strange some unknown creature would pop up here.

Ten miles away in Oceana, thirty-nine-year-old Patrolman Bill Pritt came face to face with a seven-foot creature in August of 1978 right in front of the Oceana Town Hall. It was an early Monday morning, dark with fog trickling through the town tucked into the forest and mountains deep in Wyoming County. Pritt was working with Chief Raymond Walker and was on the tail end of a twelve-hour shift—7 p.m. to 7 a.m. when dispatch received a call. A baby was screaming in a neighborhood near the Oceana Town Hall. Pritt was the closest officer to the area, and he got into his cruiser and drove to the location along Monroe Street.

"I radioed the jail and told them I'd be out of the car checking on some babies crying," Pritt disclosed not long after. "I checked this trailer, and the man said it was probably cats fighting. We couldn't find any evidence of a catfight, so we started to check the neighborhood to find out where the weird sound was coming from. It let out a squall that scared me to death. I mean, the hairs on the back of my neck stood straight up. I've never heard anything like it."

Pritt was a seasoned cop; he thought he had probably seen everything. "I went on down toward Johnny Aliff's house," he went on, "and I saw what I thought was a man standing under a street light. I noticed that it was big, but he didn't move to hide from me, and with that noise, it wasn't really usual for somebody to be out there." Pritt divulged, stating it turned around with its back to him. "Then it kind of leaped and I hollered at it. I thought it was somebody who'd been into something and was trying to get away from me, and it had jumped down over the bank to the edge of the river." Pritt shined a spotlight along the Clear Fork but saw nothing. "It had jumped completely across the river. It had to have jumped because I didn't hear any splashing, and as close as I was, I would have heard if it had hit the water," Pritt stated. "I saw it moving up the bank on the other side, and I fired six shots at it. After that, I just don't remember. I was scared to death." It did not stop the beast that disappeared into the forest.

Clear Fork River runs behind the neighborhood. Dense brush covers most of the banks throughout the town proper.

It was difficult for locals, DNR, and town officials to digest. They tried to call it a misplaced heron. But Pritt was adamant what he saw was no bird. "It was dark-colored, and it looked like a man. A bird has spindly legs, and a crane would have a long neck. This didn't have either. It was like a man, only big, and it must have weighed three-hundred-pounds. You can laugh at me and think I'm crazy if you want, but I saw it, and I don't want to see it again," the officer responded.

And there was no concern he was a credible witness; the Oceana Town Recorder was steadfast in the statement the man was a level-headed officer. Oceana Police Chief Raymond Walker, who heard Pritt's shots and made his way to the river, told reporters: "I don't think it could hurt you, because it's had the opportunity to attack, and it hasn't. It's moved away, so I don't think anybody should fear for their safety." Pritt was not so convinced. "Maybe not," Pritt answered quickly, "but if I see it again, I'm sure not going to go up to it and try to start a conversation."

Most would agree with Pritt. Of course, for those like me who eagerly went looking for it in downtown Oceana and deeper into the dark woodlands of Poke Holler at Twin Falls and along Polk Gap Road where it abuts all things dark and mysterious, it evaded me. For today, that is. There is always tomorrow.

Where can you find a Polk Gap/Poke Hollow Monster?

Take a drive from Oceana (37.692525, -81.633378) to Twin Falls Resort State Park (37.636819, -81.439062)

Polk Gap—where the road ends and into private property. What beast lurking beyond is only left to the imagination of those of us who cannot enter.

Poke Hollow Trail and Poke Holler—Twin Falls State Park—Off Park Road 803 (Poke Hollow Road), Mullens, WV.
Parking: (37.645601, -81.431986) —The full trail is 3.5 miles— eerie, serene, and beautiful. If you don't see the Poke Holler Monster here, you'll walk out feeling like maybe IT saw you. You can walk all or just a little.

*For those wondering if **Polk** and **Poke** might just be a mispronunciation of the same name—I don't know. There were Poke and Polk families in the region. Regardless—to the right is the Poke Hollow Trail. There are 2 little lights on the image. I had them show up in a couple pictures. They could be reflections of spiders or insects along the trail. Or more to my liking, a ghost. Someone mentioned to me that Poke Hollow was also haunted!*

West Virginia

Bigfoot-*Ghillie Beast*

Seneca Rocks

Description: 7-10 feet tall. Dark. Bigfoot-like.

Other Names: Bigfoot. Ghillie Beast.

Location: Seneca Rocks, WV and surrounding byways—Pendleton County, WV

View of twisty-turny roads from Seneca Rocks observation platform. A great place to see mountains—and Bigfoot. Trail: 1.3 miles (2.6 miles round-trip)

The mountain roads near Seneca Rocks are twisty with sheer drop-offs and only a flimsy guardrail between a front bumper and being airborne over the treetops. The steep grade is hardly suitable for the semi-trucks bearing heavy loads and tearing down the backroads like it is the straight open highway. But they do.

Not me. I am suddenly a teetotaling granny who only drives on Sunday mornings to church. I drive mountain roads often and twisty-turny ones, at that. Still, there is something about Route 55 and that dang horseshoe curve that gets me every time. I am continually pulling off, with the prim airs of a Sunday driver, for locals who have the route down. Regardless, drivers should slow down a little—there have been some Bigfoot sightings along that road and into the Monongahela National Forest at Seneca Rocks. A couple taking a longcut back to Ohio at about 11:30 p.m. on a Sunday spotted a six-foot, hairy creature in the high beam lights of the car behind them. On a late afternoon, around 4:30 p.m., a hiker at Seneca Rocks observed a Bigfoot. It was about seven feet tall with matted orange-brown hair almost a foot long.

On a chilly and rainy January night, a man towing a U-Haul observed an ape-like creature near the road not far from Seneca Rocks. It appeared to be covered in gray and black matted hair, had no neck, and had a huge head. He first thought it was a hunter in a woodland camouflage ghillie suit with cloth and twine dangling to look like leaves and twigs. The driver whipped the car around and pulled into a drive for a better look. With a flick of his flashlight, he scanned the wooded area and saw nothing. But he heard a lot—squeals and grunts and wood hitting together. Then, there was silence.

Where can you look for Ghillie Beast at Seneca Rocks?

Seneca Rocks Trailhead—
WV-28 N/WV-55 E,
Seneca Rocks, WV 26884
(38.835717, -79.372418)

Monsters of Ohio

Monster/Cryptid	Map #
Bigfoot	
Cleveland Metro Parks Rocky River	1
Cuyahoga Valley National Park	2
Salt Fork State Park	3
Hocking Hills Region	4
Wild Man of Gallipolis	5
Minerva Monster	6
Loveland Frogman	7
Ohio River Sea Serpent	8
Crosswick Monster	9

Monster/Cryptid	Map #
Cedar Bog Monster	10
Devil Monkey	11
Delphos Dogman	12
Defiance Werewolf	13
Charles Mill Lake—Green-Eyed Monster	14
Charles Mill Lake—Orange Eyes	15
Peninsula Python	16
Camp Manatoc Red Eyes	17
Melon Heads	18
South Bay Bessie	19

Ohio

Bigfoot

Cleveland Metro Parks Rocky River/ Rocky River Reservation

Description: Bipedal, primate-like creature. Dark skin. Thick brow. Broad shoulders.

Names: Bigfoot. Grassman.

Location: Cleveland Metroparks—Rocky River Reservation in Oh—Cuyahoga County

Cleveland Metroparks—Rocky River Reservation where two people fishing caught sight of a Bigfoot—This trail begins across from the Rocky River Nature Center and along the bridle trail. (41.408752, -81.883858)

Two women were fishing around 5:00 p.m. at Cleveland Metroparks Rocky River Reservation in Cuyahoga County.

They were settled in on a rock wall when the sound of deer crossing the river caught their attention. They saw movement in the woods across from them only five minutes later, about twenty feet away. At first, it appeared to be a white-tailed deer standing on its hind legs eating leaves. As the sunlight fell on the animal, it exposed a face with strange, glowing red-orange eyes staring at them.

As it worked its way out of the woods, the two realized it was not a deer but a towering black figure trudging along on two legs. It had dark skin, a thick brow, and dark hair slightly longer on the shoulders. It was huge, bigger than a grown man, and with shoulders much broader than a man. Both women stood agape, then grabbed up their fishing gear and ran to their cars.

Where can you look for Bigfoot in Cleveland Metroparks?

Cleveland Metroparks—Rocky River Reservation—I would suggest stopping in at the nature center for maps and trail info: 24000 Valley Parkway, North Olmsted, OH 44070 (41.408752, -81.883858) This is along the **bridle trail**.

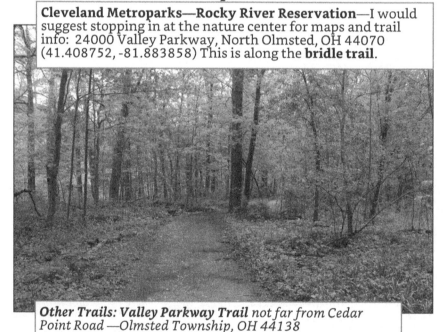

Other Trails: Valley Parkway Trail not far from Cedar Point Road —Olmsted Township, OH 44138 (41.404247, -81.884103)

There are trails that are wheelchair accessible including the Valley Parkway Trail— (41.407447, -81.882808)

Ohio

Bigfoot

Cuyahoga Valley National Park

Description: Bipedal, primate-like creature. Little to no neck. Deep brow.

Names: Bigfoot. Grassman.

Location: Cuyahoga Valley National Park —Cuyahoga County and Summit County, Oh

People have been crossing paths with hairy bipedal creatures around the 52-square mile Cuyahoga Valley National Park for years. There have been intermittent findings of tracks, occasional sightings, and recordings of howls even as recently as 2015. From watching with awe as a hairy man runs near the hike/bike trail off Sagamore Road in Sagamore Hills to hearing the distinctive howl echo near Hemlock Point, Bigfoot has been making lots of believers out of disbelievers in Northern Ohio. But who could expect anything less with the vast population of humans at the park?

In July of 1995, several hikers were trekking near the Jaite Trailhead late at night not far from the Brandywine Ski Resort and near the Cuyahoga River. In the distance, a high-pitched, coyote-like scream broke the air. They hiked a little longer, passing a swamp then decided to turn around toward their vehicle.

An immensely powerful growl broke loose into the air for about eight to ten seconds. It was close, so close. Dumbfounded, the group froze. Then came a creature running upright on two legs in the swampy water, and swinging its arms charged through the swamp straight at the group. It was not more than a silhouette, but they could see it had a round head, little to no neck, and broad shoulders. Although it was chest-deep, this massive three-hundred-pound creature was moving rapidly, cutting through the water, brush, and cattails. Instinct took over. The hikers retreated and ran back toward their vehicles, occasionally turning to see if the beast followed.

Where can you look for Bigfoot in Cuyahoga Valley National Park?

-**At Jaite Trailhead where a Bigfoot was seen and heard**—You can hop on a bit of the **Buckeye Trail**, Ohio's 1,444-mile hiking trail that loops around Ohio. Or you can also take a hike on the **Valley Bridle Trail**. Bring bug spray and wear boots—some places are a bit sloppy simply because of the type of terrain. Jaite Trailhead off Vaughn Road, Brecksville, OH 44141 (41.288845, -81.571828)

-Just up the street, you can park and walk the **Ohio and Erie Canal Towpath Trail** along the Cuyahoga River: **Red Lock Trailhead**, Northfield, OH 44067 (41.289809, -81.563872)

At Cuyahoga Valley National Park, howls were recorded at **Hemlock Point** *(below) by Bigfoot Field Researchers Association's Charlie Page (Ohio BFRO) in 2015. You can park at the* **Oakwood Trailhead** *3901 Oak Hill Road, Peninsula, OH 44264 (41.219688, -81.576110) Take the Plateau Trail to Hemlock Point. Take a current map as the trails intersect multiple times. Bigfoot have been sighted often by locals on Plateau Trail.*

To Hemlock Point

Brandywine Gorge Trail Loop—Stanford Road, Northfield, OH 44067 (41.276812, -81.540163). 1.4 miles. Or a quick walk from the parking lot.

Stanford Trail to Brandywine Falls—*For a little longer hike, park at the Boston Store Visitor Center (41.262833, -81.558474) and take the Ohio/ Erie Towpath Trail to the Stanford Trail (Trailhead: hike 2.25 miles to Brandywine Falls.) There have been reports of sightings and howls.*

Boston Store Visitor Center and Canal Towpath Trail.

Stanford Trail, left.

Brandywine Falls Trail, right.

Ohio

Bigfoot

Salt Fork State Park

Description: Bipedal, primate-like creature. Very dark.

Names: Bigfoot. Grassman.

Location: Salt Fork State Park—Guernsey County, Oh

Hosak's Cave—one of Salt Fork State Park's many natural areas where Bigfoot has been sighted and has placed it at the top of the list of areas Bigfoot can be found. In 1978, 1979, and 1987 a 6-foot female creature with dark brown hair was sighted near Hosacks Cave, a 60-foot-high sandstone cliff with a rocky overhang. Vocalizations and rock throwing. The lower trail, accessible off Park Road No. 1. Hosak's Cave—Salt Fork State Park Kimbolton, OH 43749 (40.135866, -81.492075) A short walk from the parking lot.

When I asked one of Ohio and West Virginia's leading Bigfoot researchers the best place to look for Bigfoot in Ohio, I got a resounding "Salt Fork State Park!" Dr. Russell Jones is a chiropractor, author, and researcher/field investigator for reported sightings for the BFRO—Bigfoot Field Researchers Organization. He has also appeared on several episodes of Animal Planet's "Finding Bigfoot" television series.

The Charleston Gazette-Mail interviewed Jones about his book—*Tracking the Stone Man: West Virginia's Bigfoot.* One point he related was this: "Probably ninety to ninety-five percent of the reports BFRO receives involve incidents that can be explained by things other than Bigfoot. But out of every hundred, there will be a couple that cannot be identified as something else and involves credible witnesses with compelling accounts who are teachers, doctors, electricians, or law enforcement officers. Some of these people have been traumatized by what they have seen. With my book, I'm not trying to convince people that Bigfoot exists — I'm just hoping to convince people to keep an open mind on the subject." He is a leading researcher in West Virginia but has explored Ohio in length also. So, when Dr. Jones said Salt Fork, I listened.

Salt Fork State Park Lodge —Bigfoot has been seen near the lodge, along Purple Loop Trail, and the offices. 14755 Cadiz Road, Cambridge, OH 43725 (40.105919, -81.529087) Lodge and Freedom Road - Whoops, knockings, vocalizations, and objects tossed at people. Bigfoot peering from behind trees.

Located in eastern Ohio, Salt Fork State Park has a whopping 17,229 acres for Bigfoot to inhabit. It has all the makings of perfect Bigfoot habitat—prey like deer, squirrels, rabbits, and plenty of available water on Salt Fork Lake. It has room to roam and plenty of places to remain hidden. Between the mid-1980s and 2018, there have been over thirty-six sightings at the park.

One of the picnic areas at the park where reports have been made of Bigfoot sightings.

In August of 2004, an ordinary picnic took a horrifying turn when a couple went for a stroll with their dog into the woods. It was a quiet evening, around 7:00. Abruptly, the two began to hear loud howls. The sound seemed to be working its way parallel to their hiking feet. After stopping to take a closer look, the man saw a nearly eight-foot-tall, dark-colored form looking at him and his wife. He was interviewed by the Daily Jeffersonian out of Cambridge, Ohio, and stated this: "What we saw —it was standing there. It was dark - I will not say it was covered with hair — but it was a dark figure standing nearly eight feet tall. I could see its head [move from side to side] like it is looking at me. And then it turns and keeps on walking [down the hill]."

Now both frightened, the couple retreated to the picnic area, grabbed their belongings, and left.

In another encounter, a couple was camping in the primitive campsites at Bigfoot Ridge. They had heard occasional screams as they started to sleep. Around 1:00 in the morning, the sound of something tearing grass from the earth awakened the woman. She waited until the noise faded away. When it quieted, she opened the door to the tent and crawled out, shining her flashlight on the surrounding area.

At the edge of the woods, she saw two large, yellowish eyes the size of golf balls staring at her. Just as quickly as they were there, they vanished. The couple promptly packed up their site and left, abandoning their tent.

The sign states: BIGFOOT RIDGE – It is the primitive camping area where there has been much activity including Bigfoot rock throwing, vocalizations, and knocks.

Bigfoot have been sighted hiding behind trees here peering at campers. Parking Area Salt Fork State Park: (40.121076, -81.508646)

Where else can you look for Bigfoot at Salt Fork?

Along the trail to Kennedy Stonehouse Museum – *Here, wood knocks have been heard, tracks have been discovered, and stones tossed. Hike .8 miles from the parking lot: R-4 Kimbolton, OH 43749 (40.131549, -81.486002)*

Kennedy Stonehouse Museum
14755 Cadiz Road, Lore City, OH 43755
(40.127862, -81.499626)

Park Road 1—Just take a drive along Park Road - Three Bigfoot have been seen along the road.

It starts about here: (40.121607, -81.496349) and runs all the way to here: (40.082388, -81.460043)

Morgan's Knob Trail—It is a 2.2-mile out-and-back trail. Hikers hear wood knocks here. Three children had a sighting of a bigfoot stalking a deer. Park Road 3 near the lodge. (40.116392, -81.526086)

The old road that is now the Morgan's Knob Trail

Pine Forest at beginning of trail. Trail signs show maps for easy access.

Doing some wood knocks with a stick found on the ground.

The trail starts on an open grassy area and quickly moves on to a thick pine forest leading into a well-defined path that was once a road, surrounded by hardwoods. It has a minimum of four different habitats accommodating many different varieties of edible vegetation (like blackberry, strawberry, morel mushrooms), birds (like cardinals, robins, hawks) and animals (like squirrels, rabbits, voles, mice) for each habitat, all good eating for bobcat, bear and—Bigfoot.

It also has an open pathway easily accessible for both hikers and animals. Like powerline right-of-ways, Bigfoot sightings tend to appear higher around these types of settings. Bigfoot are believed to be opportunists—it is easier to walk through maintained areas than march through thorny wild rose and ankle-catching, skin-lashing brier.

When I searched up old maps, I found out that it was an old road that was probably pretty busy for its time in the 1800s and early 1900s. Along the route were many homes and farms like the Clarks, the Wrights, and the Leepers. There was even the Covenanter Church nearby. While you take the trail, you will see some old foundations and remnants of the past. With so much to offer, it is the perfect place for big creatures to hang out, and it is probably the reason this area is one of the top spots in the park to be lucky enough to catch a sighting of Bigfoot. There have been tracks discovered, growls heard, Bigfoot peering behind trees, and wood knocks.

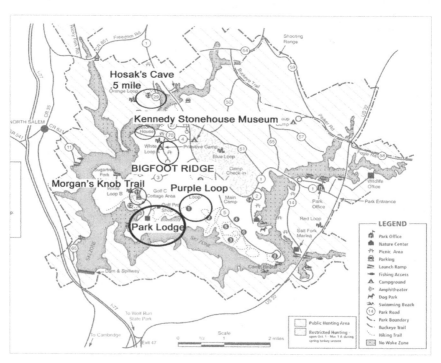

Ohio

Bigfoot-*Grassman*

Hocking Hills Region

Description: Bipedal, primate-like creature.

Names: Bigfoot. Grassman.

Location: Ash Cave-Hocking Hills State Park—Hocking County, Oh

Hocking Hills State Park is visited by over five million tourists a year. They seek out the unique terrain—the recess caves, the cliffs, and the deep pockets of old forest. Sometimes, they find more than they expected. There have been Bigfoot sightings between Logan and Old Man's Cave and many reports of knocking and banging by campers at both private and state park campgrounds. Along the popular park trails, it may not be easy to differentiate between the noises that hikers make and the sounds of a foraging creature. Still, the area is extensive with forests, natural areas, and national forests. Most parts of Hocking and nearby Vinton County are not heavily trafficked by humans—especially outside of summer and fall. Hocking Hills State Park is also strict about hikers staying directly on the trails—it is against the law to go off-trail because of the dangerous cliffs. When the parks close at dusk, the silence is deafening.

Rose Lake is near the Hocking Hills State Park Campground. By day, it can be busy with hikers and folks fishing. But when evening rolls in, it is pretty quiet. The perfect time, perhaps, for Bigfoot to come and fish out some stocked fish too.

Rose Lake: *You can access Rose Lake with a 1/2 mile hike from the parking lot off Route 374: (39.432044, -82.528346)*

No trails seem to compete better for Bigfoot sightings than the region between Ash Cave and Rose Lake. A hilly path leads through the Hocking State Forest located between the two with hemlocks and massive beech trees. Along the way, there are meandering creeks and old logging roads. It was one of these very paths hunters were using when one had a very startling experience with a Bigfoot!

Four men were hunting in a designated hunting area in autumn in the forestry area between Cedar Falls and Ash Cave. They broke off into a couple of different parties. While one group worked their way along a trail, one man began to smell something putrid like rotting meat. Scoffing if off as nothing more than decaying vegetation, they continued onward. Along the way, they noticed a bare footprint, which was decidedly strange for October.

In the afternoon, there was rustling in the brush. One of the men decided to check it out, descending the hill before he stopped. To his surprise, he saw something he could not quite fathom even for an experienced hunter—a seven-foot-tall ape-like creature covered with dark brown hair and having a human-like nose, thick brow ridges, and a sloped forehead. He hastily returned and said it was time to leave. Returning on following hunting seasons, he would have additional sightings, find footprints, and even hear a growl.

Hocking State Forest between Cedar Falls and Ash Cave. You can park at Cedar Falls. There is a trail that leads into the Hocking State Forest beyond the Cedar Falls picnic shelter—(39.418765, -82.525870)

Where can you track Bigfoot in the Hocking Hills?

Hike from Ash Cave to Cedar Falls— One way—2.5 miles. Ash Cave Parking: State Route 56, South Bloomingville, OH 43152 (39.396088, -82.545740) Or hike Rose Lake: At Rose Lake, a father and son came face to face with a hairy, ape-like creature while walking the trail around the lake. The father reported the event to park officers, who immediately scanned the area but found no evidence.

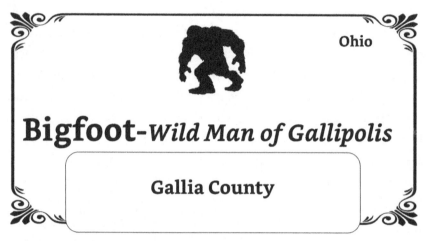

Ohio

Bigfoot-*Wild Man of Gallipolis*

Gallia County

Description: Covered in hair. Eyes are bulging.
Other Names: Bigfoot.
Location: Gallipolis, Oh—Gallia County

In January of 1869, a man and his daughter were driving a carriage near Gallipolis. A wild naked, hairy man, huge in size, bounded out into the carriage path and attacked the father. He took the man in a vise-like grip, lifted him high, and hurled him to the ground. Then the beastly creature fell atop him and attempted to bite and scratch the man while they rolled in the muddy carriage path.

The man fought but became overwhelmed and exhausted. His daughter picked up a rock and hurled it at the head of the wild man, and her daring act seemed enough to startle the creature into submission. He stopped, appeared stunned, and slowly clambered off into a thicket skirting the road.

Occasionally, there are Bigfoot reports in the surrounding areas of Gallipolis, including Cheshire. Motorists have seen a large, hairy creature along the Ohio River. In 1998, two campers near Hoadley Road and Wayne National Forest in Gallia County witnessed what they could only surmise was a Bigfoot coming into their camping spot.

They listened as twigs snapped and flashed a light into the darkness of night to see a pair of blue eyes nearly eight feet off the ground. The next morning, they found large human-like footprints in the soil.

Hoadley Road at Wayne National Forest.

Where can you look for the Wild Man of Gallipolis?

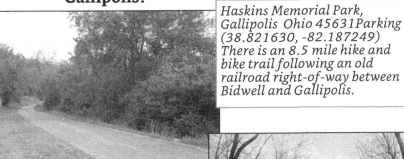

Haskins Memorial Park, Gallipolis Ohio 45631 Parking (38.821630, -82.187249) There is an 8.5 mile hike and bike trail following an old railroad right-of-way between Bidwell and Gallipolis.

Symmes Wildlife Area and Wayne National Forest Waterloo, OH 45688 (38.719660, -82.498115)

Bigfoot-*Minerva Monster*

Minerva

Description: Matted hair. Stubby legs. Eyes flash red in a flashlight beam.

Other Names: The Big Hairy Thing.

Location: Minerva, Oh—Columbiana and Stark Counties

Minerva, Ohio—Home to the Minerva Monster.

When it arrived, the crickets and frogs silenced themselves, and the air stank like stagnant water. It was the calm before the storm, and a family from Minerva, Ohio, was thrust into the eye of that storm in August of 1978.

Something must have stirred IT up, the THING they saw—the huge thing with matted hair and stubby legs—*the Big Hairy Thing.*

It may have happened when Herbert Cayton (age 60) and his wife Evelyn (age 55) cleared some brush behind their home and around an abandoned strip mine. They had done so to open up the area—there had been a rash of thefts and strange sounds in the neighborhood. Cleaning out the overgrowth left no place for vandals to hide. They were disturbed after they cut the brush and peered to the newly cleared area, it appeared a large animal like a deer, or worse, someone BIG had been laying on a patch of mashed-down underbrush. It was not typical, that is for sure.

A few nights later, the Cayton's grandchildren and some neighborhood kids, ranging from four to twelve years old, were playing outside. They burst through the door, utterly terrified and crying. Something was out there, something big—almost six feet tall and covered with matted fur.

Evelyn Cayton, her twenty-six-year-old daughter Vicki Keck, and her son, eighteen-year-old Howie, ran out to the banks of the old strip mine pit. They stood there in awe—only fifty feet away, they were staring eye-to-eye. "It just stood there," Evelyn told reporters later. "It didn't move, but I about broke my neck running down the hill." She saw it again in daylight, and it was squatting down by the old strip mine pit.

It would only be a couple of days later—about 10:30 on a Monday night when Evelyn, her daughter, and three visitors were sitting on the porch and heard some racket by a rickety chicken coop. They set out to investigate the noise with a flashlight. There was something inside. When the flashlight beam slipped through the darkness, they could see two sets of large, glowing eyes in the beam. A larger creature stepped in front of a smaller one as if protecting it.

The area where the Minerva Monster was seen. Most of the land around Minerva is private property, especially in the zone of the initial sightings. That said, you'll have to stick with driving the byways around the town if you want to search out the monster—

Eighteen-year-old Scott Patterson, a visiting friend of the family, hopped into his car, worked his way up the drive, and shined the headlights on the coop. The larger creature broke through the lights and made a lurching amble toward the car. Five outside watching ran pell-mell into the house, a hasty retreat only harboring them from immediate danger. They called the police. While waiting around the kitchen table, the creature stood outside the window for ten minutes while Evelyn snatched up a rifle and aimed it at the glass. Scott Patterson held a pistol. One of the visitors, Mary, would admit it did not seem to want to bother anyone. It appeared curious. It finally disappeared into the dark.

Others would see this monster standing on the hill not far from the home or in the thick woodlands around the town. The shadowy form that wandered around the house and tossed rocks at the windows would also howl out in the black of night. It seemed to scare everything else away. Deer, turkey, and rabbits vanished when it was around.

It would not be the first time the creature showed. Earlier, Howie, his brother, and three friends set off to find IT in the woods and tried to tackle it. Howie would tell a Fox 8 News Crew in Cleveland, "It actually threw us off like we were just little kids. It actually bit my brother. My brother, he probably had a three-inch bite mark on his shoulder—" It was like a human bite, but it didn't break the skin. The creature effortlessly jumped a large bank and went off into the woods.

The night it all started, the family called the Stark County Sheriff's Department. Captain Jim Shannon arrived on the scene and scouted out the area. He immediately smelled an ammonia-sulfur scent. The captain saw the horror in their eyes. But he did not find much more than a bit of hair the department sent off for testing and was lost. But the story hit the newspapers. The Caytons took a certain amount of ridicule for what they saw. People from all over came to find what would be called The Minerva Monster. The police combed the countryside while helicopters hovered overhead. Reporters and curiosity seekers scoured the area. Hunters came by the droves with dogs and rifles and the desire to kill it. Nobody found it. And eventually, the story faded into old newspapers. But not so for the Minerva Monster. Sometimes folks at the nearby trailer park catch a glimpse of it on the road or hear the rocks pelt the siding of their mobile homes. "Whatever it is, it's not dangerous," Evelyn would tell Barbara Mudak, a staff writer with The Akron Beacon Journal, later. "If it was going to hurt someone, it would have done it by now."

Where can you look for the Minerva Monster?

The area where witnesses saw the monster is private property. But you can take a drive down public roads around town!

Ohio

Loveland Frogman

Loveland's Cold-blooded Cryptid

Description: Brow-less eyes. Grayish color. Large straight mouth so long, it spans completely across the face. Froglike. No apparent lip muscles. Bald head—ribbed almost appearing like a plastic baby doll with ridged, painted hair. The upper torso is lopsided, unmatching.

Other Names: Shawnahooc.

Location: Loveland, Oh—Hamilton, Clermont, and Warren Counties

A Frogman once showed up in the headlights of cars in Loveland.

When folks think of the Loveland Frogman, they tend only to conjure up the 1972 hoax perpetrated by local Loveland policeman Mark Matthews whose confession stunned the city in 2016. It all started with a different cop— at 1:00 a.m. on a chilly March 3rd morning in 1972, police officer Ray Shockey was driving along Riverside Road and spotted something odd near the Totes Boot Factory not far from the Little Miami River. He thought it was a dog before it stood up on two legs. It clambered over the guardrail and headed down an embankment on two feet and into the Little Miami. He would describe the creature as about four feet tall, sixty pounds, and having leathery skin. His sister even did a composite drawing of what Shockey saw—a man-sized frog clambering over a guardrail. It shook him up.

He called another officer, Mark Matthews, and confided his story to him. Later that month, Matthews took Kemper Road near the boot factory and saw something odd beneath the guardrail. He stopped and eyed the creature. The trigger-happy cop also pulled out his gun, and Matthews let the bullets fly. "I know no one would believe me, so I shot it," he confessed to a WCPO Cincinnati reporter nearly forty-four years later, after quickly adding it was a sickly iguana. "The thing was half dead anyway when I shot it." He said he dumped it in the trunk of his cruiser and drove off, showing it to Shockey, who said it was the creature he had seen. "It's a big hoax," he said. "There's a logical explanation for everything."

Logical? Iguanas can grow over five feet long, although that is from nose to tip of the tail. They seldom run around on two legs and jump guardrails. The odds that they would are about the same as a man-size frog strolling up and down the shores of the Little Miami River because the Central and South American iguanas are sluggish at fifty degrees.

Anything less, and the warm climate iguanas become stunned and freeze up. In Miami Beach, Florida, during a weird cold snap in 2018 where temperatures dropped to forty degrees, iguanas perched in the trees froze and fell to the ground. The low temperature on March 2nd, when Ray Shockey saw the creature take off under the guardrail, was a drizzly twenty-seven degrees. The high that day barely made it to sixty degrees. On March 17th, when Matthews killed the strange critter, the high was barely forty-eight degrees. Logical? Maybe, maybe not. Because it was not the first time that passersby had seen the creature—and this time, by credible witnesses—

Loveland, Ohio, is settled into the western side of Ohio, a suburb of Cincinnati described as having a small-town atmosphere with a large city feel. It has more than one historic district, some with distinguished older homes and others with bike trails, cafes, and ice cream shops. The Little Miami River runs through it, along with a bit of the popular seventy-mile Little Miami State Park bike trail, following an old railway line of the Little Miami Steam Railroad chartered in 1836.

In the 1700s, along the Little Miami, there lived Native Indians-The Miami (Mihtohseeniaki, The People), also called the Twightwee by nearby Delaware. Here, the story of the real Loveland Frogman is said, by many, to begin. For among those early tribes living on the Little Miami shores, there was a legend that was passed on to French settlers of the *Shawnahooc*—a human-like creature with wrinkled skin and lacking a nose and living within the waters. They spoke of a party of hunters returning to their home that came across the demon-like monster, and even as they shot at it, the creature jumped into the water unharmed.

For a couple hundred years, they warded the monster off. But it returned about 4:00 a.m. on May 25th, 1955.

Robert Hunnicutt, a short-order chef for a newly opened restaurant, was driving northeast through Branch Hill (in Symmes Township) on the Loveland-Madeira Pike near Hopewell Road. As he zipped over a rise and was coming down a slight grade, in the beam of his headlights, Hunnicutt caught the image of a group of figures. They appeared to be kneeling along the right side of the road in the berm with their backs to the brush.

The vicinity of Loveland-Madeira Road where Hunnicutt's sighting took place.

His first impression was that the men were praying. Believing it strange, Hunnicutt brought his car to a halt and pulled over to the side. As realization washed over him, Hunnicutt was stunned to see that the figures were not human at all—they stood erect and were only about three and a half feet high. Hunnicutt got out of the left side of his car, noting that the central form of the three was holding both hands in the air and brandishing dark chains or rods from which blue-white sparks jumped from hand to hand. All three seemed focused across the road and not at Hunnicutt, as if signaling something in the woods.

When Hunnicutt progressed farther, the figure's arms lowered, and it appeared to tie whatever it was holding in its hands around its ankles. Suddenly, all three figures turned slightly left and toward him simultaneously. They stared directly at him with brow-less eyes—the creatures being of grayish color with large straight mouths so long, they spanned completely across the face—frog-like, and with no apparent lip muscles. The creatures' heads were bald, ribbed, like a plastic baby doll with ridged, painted-on hair. Their upper torsos seemed lopsided and unmatched.

So curious was Hunnicutt, he approached the frog-like creatures near the fender of his car. He would have been about ten feet away. It was then the figures made an odd but graceful motion that Hunnicutt felt was a warning for him to stop his steps. He would stand there another few minutes before a feeling washed over him—the whole event was truly inconceivable. Frightened that he had been so mesmerized by the bizarre scene and he had forgotten his safety, he jumped back into his car and drove immediately to Police Chief John Fritz's home, banging frantically at the front door. Later, Chief Fritz would state, "He looked as if he'd seen a ghost." Although he was an acquaintance of Hunnicutt, the story seemed just too unreal, straight down to the scent that had enveloped him as he drove away—something akin to fresh-cut alfalfa with a slight trace of almonds. He leaned in enough to catch a bit of Hunnicutt's breath and smelled no scent of beer on it. Satisfied the man was not drunk, the police chief sent Hunnicutt home, then plopped his gun in his belt and snatched up a camera to investigate this incredible report. He found nothing peculiar.

Leonard Stringfield was a well-known American ufologist who researched and collected dozens of stories from persons not only associated with the government, but also knowledgeable of the government's hidden UFO data.

He must have felt there was a tie between these creatures and aliens as he interviewed local civil defense authorities. He found that Hunnicutt had seen the frog-like entities at approximately the same time that a couple not far away would have a strange occurrence. In a subdivision of Loveland called Loveland Heights, whose lower corridors of South and Mid Heights run about a half-mile parallel to the river, Emily Magnone and her husband were awakened on a hot summer night with a start by their dog's frantic barking outside. They arose and peered out the windows and saw nothing. However, a rank, swampy odor filled their nostrils. It became so overpowering; they had to close the windows even though their house was already hot. Still, the smell persisted, seeming to cling to the fabric of the house. The next morning while chatting with a neighbor, Missus Magnone learned the neighbor, too, had peeked outside the night before. And she saw the strangest thing—a tiny man covered entirely in leaves and twigs who stood still and stared at her. When Missus Magnone flipped the lights on, it would disappear. When turned off, she could make out the faint outline of the little man again.

Stringfield was a persistent man. He also found a fourth witness (through the local police chief) to the strange Frogman. Of course, Stringfield was willing to bet the creature in question could be an alien. The witness was a nineteen-year-old Civil Defense worker, an auxiliary policeman, whose name was only given as C.F. for anonymity. He was wary, suspicious, and unwilling to answer many questions due to the ridicule he received at work when divulging he saw the creatures.

In the early summer of 1955, the witness had been driving a civil defense truck across a bridge. For a mere ten seconds, C.F. had caught a glimpse of some strange beings.

He described these creatures as "four more-or-less human-looking little men about three feet high that had been moving about oddly under the bridge, and that there had been a terrible smell about the place."

Loveland Avenue Bridge over the Little Miami River where the human-sized frog was seen. You can try your luck at finding it at Bishop City Park—1424 W Loveland Avenue, Loveland, OH 45140 (39.268538, -84.261391)

Where else can you look for the Frogman?

So, there are the stories, hoaxes aside. Maybe you can come up with your own experience. You can walk the Loveland bike path from the East Loveland Nature Preserve and for about a mile and a half stretch, enjoy the scenery, and maybe get a sighting of the Frogman as its path of sightings parallels (from the opposite side) the Little Miami River where witnesses saw the creature.

Parking for the Loveland Bike Path: Walk the bike path along the Little Miami River—Downtown Loveland, OH 45140 (39.266364, -84.259658) (Walk away from the downtown) about 1.6 miles to here: Little Miami Scenic Trail Loveland, OH 45140 (39.251630, -84.281877) 10078 E Kemper Road, Loveland, OH 45140. The latter is just about across from the area where the old Totes Factory was located.

Ohio

Ohio River Sea Serpent

Cincinnati Serpent

Description: 12–15 feet long. Serpent-like head. Covered in black, glossy substance. Hide akin to alligator skin.

Other Names: Sea Serpent.

Location: Roebling Suspension Bridge—Cincinnati, Oh—Hamilton County. Covington, KY—Kenton County

It is always when you least expect it, right—? When you are merrily going along your way. Regardless, this is the Roebling Suspension Bridge between Covington and Cincinnati. You can walk across it. It is a nice adventure—if you are not afraid of heights and serpents.

On Friday, January 11th, 1878, Ben Karrick saw a sea serpent in the Ohio River. It was right beneath the Roebling Suspension Bridge where his delivery wagon was working its way across. He guessed it as being twelve to fifteen feet long and with the head of an enormous serpent. A black glossy substance like hair covered the body, and the skin was like the hard hide of an alligator. It lashed its tail several times and moved fast, hissing and making a deep bellow much like a cow's low. He compared it to a huge seahorse.

Where can you look for the Ohio River Sea Serpent?

You can walk across the Roebling Suspension Bridge—Public Parking:
62-16 Riverside Drive
Covington, KY 41011
(39.090812, -84.509563)

Ohio

Crosswick Monster

An Ohio Dragon

Description: 30-40 feet long. 16 inches in diameter. Legs 4 feet long and giving it the ability to stand erect and propel tail. Tail. Covered in scales. Black and white with wide, yellow spots. Feet shaped like a lizard and 12 inches long. Head —16 inches wide. Long, black forked tongue. Red mouth.

Other Names: Snaix.

Location: Crosswick, Oh—Warren County

One of the Midwest's prime antique shopping towns, Waynesville, was an early Quaker settlement along the Little Miami River. These Quakers left their homes in southern states in opposition to slavery. It was isolated farmland and woods, far enough from the large cities of Columbus and Cincinnati to provide a safe and quiet haven for its townspeople. But over the years, it grew and prospered along with a community called Crosswick just a mile north on Bellbrook Road, where nearly forty-five African Americans also built a small but thriving town.

It is Crosswick where a strange story arose. Nine-year-old Joe and fourteen-year-old Ed Lynch set out to fish at a small creek, Satterthwaites Run, south of their home in Crosswick. They stopped along the bank and set up poles.

They launched lines into the water and settled in, chattering. Until that is, they heard the scratching sound of reeds and brush moving. Both turned and took in their breaths, horrified—a huge lizard-like *monster*!

The place where Satterthwaites Run crosses Old Stage Road in Crosswick and near the area the boys saw the monster.

They dropped their poles then stood paralyzed while the stuff of horrible nightmares came rushing through the reeds. The lizard was ten times their size, with legs as tall as the oldest boy. It dragged a tail and was black and white and covered with yellow spots. A forked tongue popped out, and they screamed. The sound seemed to awaken something in the monster because it reached out two clawed arms and snatched the elder of the two boys in its grasp. Then in only a matter of seconds, it dragged Ed about one-hundred yards down the creek to a big sycamore with a hollow base and a hole in the side and thrust him inside.

The boy's screams caught the attention of three men quarrying stone not far away—Reverend Jacob Horn, George Peterson, and Allen Jordan. The trio followed the cries and came across the monster standing at the gaping hole in the tree and grasping poor Ed. It paused and dropped the boy.

The men snatched him up and fled, summoning the local doctor and a posse who would help them pursue this beast.

It was not long before a crowd of men gathered at the sycamore with hounds and axes and clubs. They started to cut the tree down, readying to battle this snake or reptile or monster. The creature was still there, but seeing the men jumped from the tree and ran off into the brush. The men made hasty chase until they nearly reached another small creek, Mill Creek, and a cave between a ledge of rocks, where it quickly disappeared. Those searching would never find the monster, even though the men blasted the cave with dynamite and removed the rubble to investigate what they hoped was the dead creature inside. The cave was empty.

The boy was severely bruised and cut, but he lived. Those who knew him said he spoke little after the event. The creature was sighted again in the Shaker Swamps not far away and years later. A 1964 Dayton Journal Herald remarked that during its era, witnesses were still sighting the strange monster at the Little Miami River. Farms in the area did have missing animals attributed to the creature. In 1978, a couple at nearby Caesar Creek State Park witnessed a creature, not unlike the Crosswick monster.

Where can you look for the Crosswick Monster?

Crosswick is a few minutes drive from Waynesville. The land nearby is private; however, you can take a 2-mile drive along Old Stage Road from the Museum at the Friends Home (39.531327, -84.089574) along Old Stage Road through Crosswick and toward the creek where the boys found the monster. (39.557260, -84.066698)

Cedar Bog Monster

Ohio

Peeping Fen Monster

Description: Red eyes. White. Bigfoot-like.
Other Names: The Fen Monster.
Location: Cedar Bog—Champaign County

In 1942, the Ohio Historical Society listed Cedar Bog near Urbana, Ohio, as a nature preserve. It is not actually a bog. Bogs do not drain. They are more like a bathtub holding water. Cedar Bog is a fen and fens drain instead of just sitting there full of water that has to evaporate to go away. Instead, it drains into Cedar Run.

That aside, it has a monster lurking around who probably does not care if it is a fen or a bog or anything for that matter. But folks have seen it. It was not long after the historical society designated it as a preserve that witnesses saw a white hairy ape-like creature lurking along Woodburn Road near the fen. There were sightings by a couple using the old road beside Cedar Bog as a lover's lane. They saw a gigantic, white creature staring in the car window at them. It made no noise, but it reeked.

There is a legend about the fence surrounding Cedar Bog. Rumors tell that a government agency placed a high chain-link fence around the fen. It was not to keep people out. Instead, they set it there to keep the monster within!

Where can you look for the Cedar Bog Monster?

Above, Cedar Bog and the road where the monster was seen. You can visit Cedar Bog or drive the road. There is a fee for walking inside the grounds, and specific operating hours. Cedar Bog Nature Preserve 980 Woodburn Rd, Urbana, OH 43078 (40.057195, -83.791934)

The fence along Woodburn Road. Was it placed there to keep the monster in? That's what some legends say!

(40.055643, -83.792301)

Or if you like to hike and want to check out the habitats around Cedar Bog proper—there is also the 18-mile hike/bike trail—

Parking right up the street from Cedar Bog: Simon Kenton Trail Woodburn Road, Urbana, OH 43078 (40.055662, -83.790942)

Or for a longer hike heading toward Cedar Bog. Parking for Simon Kenton Trail: Simon Kenton Trail Off Lewis B. Moore Road, Urbana, OH 43078 (40.090554, -83.780975) And walk about 2.5 miles (one-way) to where it passes Cedar Bog—824-846 Woodburn Road, Urbana, OH 43078 (40.055535, -83.791026) The trail is paved and wheelchair/stroller accessible.

Ohio

Devil Monkey

Iron Furnace Devil Monkey

Description: Thick body. Low, squatty legs. Long tail.

Other Names: Devil.

Location: Was seen at several iron furnaces during the 1800s, most notoriously the Vesuvius Iron Furnace—Ironton, Oh—Lawrence County

Lake Vesuvius Iron Furnace where a Devil Monkey appeared.

In March of 1875, a man from Long Creek, which runs along State Route 141, was taking a longcut home past Vesuvius Iron Furnace. He heard thrashing in some bushes.

Suddenly, a thickly built creature with squatty legs and a long tail burst out into his path.

He was so startled that he could not move. But as quickly as the creature had appeared, it disappeared. Around midnight on a balmy June 26th, 1997, in Dunkinsville, Ohio, a woman saw a hairy animal with a tail, three to four feet tall, walking on its back legs and using its knuckles to help propel it forward.

Locals called it Devil Monkey, and it would not be the only sighting of this strange creature. In 1959 the Boyd family drove near Saltville, Virginia, when a monkey-like creature started after their car. "It had light, taffy-colored hair—" a passenger in the vehicle stated. "—with a white blaze down its neck and underbelly… it stood on two, large well-muscled back legs and had shorter front legs or arms." It also left scratches along the side of the vehicle. Not long after, two nurses traveling in the area in a convertible were stalked by the Devil Monkey.

Where can you look for the Devil Monkey?

Site of the 1875 sighting:
Lake Vesuvius Pedro, OH 45659
(38.605737, -82.629577)

Delphos Dogman

Ohio

Black Swamp Beasts

Description: Hairy. Half-man, Half-dog. Fangs.

Other Names: Dogman.

Location: Delphos, Oh—Allen County

It is passed down that werewolf-like, half-men and half-dogs lived along the Auglaize River during the time of the Great Black Swamp.

Glaciers once covered the area of Northwestern Ohio. Granted, it was 20,000 years ago, but when the ice finally melted, it formed the Great Lakes along with an immense wetland area called the Great Black Swamp running from Sandusky, Ohio, and as far west as Fort Wayne, Indiana.

It included parts of Allen, VanWert, and Putnam counties—and the small town of Delphos, Ohio. The land was not the best place to live. Water could be waist-high and mucky in some areas and ankle-deep in others, covered in thick brush. Malaria-carrying mosquitos flooded the region, and there were sporadic cougars, bears, and wolves. Occasionally, a werewolf would turn up, which locals dubbed Dogmen. They were most likely able to thrive because it was such a horrible place for humans to live and such, hunt it down like the rest of the predators wiped out in the areas. Old-timers have long passed down these Dogmen would hang out along the Auglaize River near the present-day Resurrection Cemetery.

Where can you look for the Delphos Dogman?

Locals tell that the Dogmen were found along the roadways crossing the Auglaize River in Delphos not far from Resurrection Cemetery which is in the rear of the picture.

Ohio

Defiance Werewolf

A Werewolf in Defiance

Description: Hunched. Wolf or Ape-like. Hairy. 6 or 7 feet tall. Wolf-teeth and fangs. Runs side to side.

Other Names: Dogman. Wolfman.

Location: Defiance, Oh—Defiance County

The tracks along Harrison Street in Defiance where the werewolf was seen. Some witnesses claimed he was wearing jeans and a t-shirt. He came out on full moon nights—

Defiance is located about fifty miles southwest of Toledo, Ohio at the confluence of the Auglaize and Maumee Rivers.

In the late 1700s, it had one of General "Mad" Anthony Wayne's forts when the U.S. was fighting against American Indian tribes. Still, it did not get many claims for fame until the railroads converged on the town in the mid-1800s. Then again in the 1970s when a werewolf came to town.

The railroads, there were two. The werewolf, only one. The werewolf snuck up on the sleepy town in July and August of 1972. It seemed to awaken the curiosity of all of those along a two-block stretch of the densely populated area near the train service depot of Defiance, Ohio. Witnesses described the creature as seven to eight feet tall and very hairy. It had fangs and raggedy clothes. The police took reports sincerely believing that it was a masked robber, at first, and not a prankster. "Very hairy is the first description given by each person who saw the 'werewolf,'" Chief Breckler of the Defiance Police told reporters. "We don't think it is a prank. He's coming at people with a club in his hand. We think it's to the safety of our people to be concerned." He also relayed two witnesses—two brakemen working the N&W local freight serving Defiance on an overnight run—Tom Jones and Ted Davis saw the beast. They stated it "had huge hairy feet, fangs, and ran from side to side, like a caveman in the movies." They also reported it had appeared twice—both under a full moon around 4 a.m.

Davis would tell the local newspaper, The Blade—"I was connecting an air hose between two cars and was looking down. I saw these huge hairy feet, then I looked up, and he was standing there with that big stick over his shoulder. When I started to say something, he took off for the woods." All of the sightings were in the wee hours of the morning. Jones, who worked in the same area and teased Davis about his sighting, saw the creature. "At first, I thought the whole thing was a big joke, but when I saw how hairy and woolly it was—that was enough for me," Jones said.

After that, reports started popping up all over town. A woman's doorknob kept rattling, and a grocery store employee who was driving home from work caught the form in his headlights at four in the morning. Others came forward who had seen the creature that had appeared to be wearing dark clothing, blue jeans, and had long fangs.

The Findlay Republican Courier announced in the August 4th, 1972 newspaper that the Defiance Werewolf might have hopped a freight train to Tiffin, a Seneca County town about seventy miles away. A man approached staff at the sheriff's office, stating he saw a "hunched, ape-like animal that was hairy, six or seven feet tall, with wolf-like teeth and fangs" while hiking in the woods. Upon seeing the creature, he took off. The local game protector scouted out the area but found no visible evidence. As the weeks went by, more people spotted the wolfman; then it appeared to vanish. The police never captured the werewolf, and the stories nearly faded away except when, once in a while, someone sees a strange wolf-man roaming an Ohio woods.

Where can you look for the Defiance Wolfman?

The train tracks are still used on Harrison in Defiance but are private property. On a full moon night, you would have to be walking the sidewalks to get a view of the wolfman— if he is still around. There have been no sightings here since 1972. Most believe he may have packed up and left town—for now.

Ohio

Green-Eyed Monster

Charles Mill Lake—Green-Eyed Monster

Description: Tall—7-feet. Green torso. Head like a fish. Lacks arms. Green eyes that glow. Flipper-like feet. Amphibious. Thin legs.

Other Names: Green-Eyed Monster of Charles Lake.

Location: Charles Mill Lake-Richland /Ashland Counties, near Mansfield *(Muskingum Watershed Conservancy District)*

It was seven feet tall, had no arms, two webbed feet, and two green eyes—as if it walked straight out of an old b-movie horror film.

Charles Mill Lake is a reservoir located in central Ohio, less than eight miles from Mansfield. It was constructed by damming the Black Fork of the Mohican River in 1935 for flood control. You can swim, fish, and boat there. I have heard you can catch some pretty big catfish at the park. Believe it or not, it is home to two strange creatures—the Green-Eyed Monster and Orange Eyes.

About the Green-Eyed Monster—they were doing what teens like to do—Denny Patterson (age 16), Wayne Armstrong (age 16), and Michael Lane (age 14)—and that was to hang out as far away as possible from adults and their rules. It was Thursday, March 26th of 1959, and they took off from their Mansfield homes and drove around for a while. A dense fog settled in, and one or the other got the idea to head to Charles Mill Lake and see how heavy that mist was coming in on the water. So they set their course to Charles Mill Lake.

The boys drove down the lane behind the boathouse. They parked the car and sat there, staring out into the dark and water. There was a log in the water, and one pointed it out. Then, it moved, stood erect. "Our hair was standing on end," Lane told reporters later. "The Thing stood up and was about seven feet tall, had no arms, two webbed feet, and two green eyes." Then it started moving toward the car.

Horrified, the driver tried to turn the car around. But it was difficult to maneuver in the small space. One of them looked out the window. The creature was fifteen feet away! The driver wrestled the car around, and the trio zoomed back to Mansfield, bursting at the seams to share their story with someone. They found a friend who scoffed at them. This insult to their credibility seemed to persuade the boys to return with a fourth passenger. And so, they did. But they were sorely disappointed. There was nothing at the lake.

On Friday, they divulged the story to Wayne Armstrong's father, who laughed at the boys' story. He suggested if they indeed saw something, it would have left some sign of its existence—maybe tracks. They returned with Wayne's father and later with a deputy from the sheriff's office. Sure enough, there were two duck-like tracks.

Where can you look for the Green-Eyed Monster?

Boat House Charles Mill Lake
1277 OH-430, Mansfield, OH 44903
(40.765048, -82.371572)

There are picnic areas overlooking the water, a campground, beach, and trails also at the park. This area is located at a point just inside the park that offers parking access and views.

Ohio

Orange Eyes

Charles Mill Lake—Orange Eye Sewer Monster

Description: Bigfoot-like. 1000 pounds. 11 feet tall. Orange, glowing eyes.

Other Names: Bigfoot. Sewer Monster.

Location: Charles Mill Lake-Richland /Ashland Counties, near Mansfield *(Muskingum Watershed Conservancy District)*

Charles Mill Lake is not only home to the Green-Eyed Monster, but also a Bigfoot-like creature and a sighting of a UFO.

Legend tells that the ape-like Orange Eyes emerged from a tunnel beneath Riverside Cemetery in Cleveland after roadway construction workers inadvertently destroyed its home. It made its path to Charles Mill Lake, where it inhabits the shallower boggy areas. Weighing in at about 1000 pounds and being eleven feet tall, it is one of Ohio's most massive and elusive creatures. Its coat is usually covered in a light fungal crust and dripping with green algae that act as camouflage. Sketchy reports come from 1963 and later on April 22nd, 1968, when children saw it and chased it with flashlights.

Where can you look for the Orange Eye Sewer Monster?

> **Charles Mill Lake**
> *1277 OH-430, Mansfield, OH 44903*
> *(40.765048, -82.371572)*

The Coyne Incident

And for those who like the UFOs, you will like what has been called The Coyne Incident, named for a pilot operating a plane that was nearly hit by a UFO near Charles Mill Lake. On October 18th, 1973, witnesses in Richland and Ashland counties reported seeing a ball of light moving plane-like and up and down in the sky. It traveled three-quarters of a mile along a roadway then disappeared. Four crew members in an Army Reserve helicopter, piloted by Lawrence Coyne, reported the plane and an unidentified flying object nearly had a collision in the vicinity of Charles Mill Lake. Witnesses on the ground verified their story. An Ashland woman saw it hovering over her backyard. It was sixty-foot-long and cigar-shaped with a bright green light.

Ohio

Peninsula Python

Travelin' Circus Snake that Got Away and Terrorized a Town

Description: 15-20 feet long. Brown and spotted.

Other Names: Giant Snake.

Location: Peninsula, Oh —Summit County

The Everett swampland where the Peninsula Python was seen. Many attributed the python's existence to a circus truck wreck—On June 18th, 1942, a King Brothers Circus truck filled with tent canvas driven by Cornelius Ford went out of control on a steep hill. It crashed into the nearby Ira Cemetery along Ira-Hammond Corners Road and smashed into the headstones, overturning. The driver was killed. Some believe that there were more than just tents in the truck.

Summit County has a snake. This alone should not be surprising; the county embraces most of Cuyahoga Valley National Park. It is the snake's size setting it apart from being a black rat snake or a corn snake common in Ohio. It is fifteen to twenty feet long, depending on with whom you chat. It is a monster of a snake that popped up in the summer of 1944, and although locals fondly dubbed the creature the *Peninsula Python*, witnesses did not see the snake in the town proper, just all the rural areas around it. Still, its appearance became legendary in Ohio, and the catchy name stuck.

Akron Peninsula Road near the Everett Swamp.

It all started with Clarence Mitchell's dogs. They had been a bit skittish for a few days. The dogs would not go out into the cornfields of his farm near Everett Swamp which was just three and a half miles south of Peninsula, Ohio, so he was on the lookout for something. However, he never expected to be on guard for the fifteen to twenty-foot long snake slithering in his cornfield near the Cuyahoga River on Wednesday, June 8th, 1944.

Mitchell told a Cleveland Press reporter this: "I don't know what made me look up, but there, about fifteen paces away, was the biggest snake I ever seen, sliding along easy and slow in plain sight on the bare ground. I just stood quiet, not aiming to attract attention. It seemed like ten minutes I watched. He slid into the river, swam across, and climbed out the other side— He was thick as my thigh, right here, and every bit of fifteen feet long—more like eighteen—sort of brownish spotted. I went over and looked at the track. It was like you'd rolled a spare tire across my field." Only a day later, a Missus Vaughn watched it eat one of her chickens whole. It was so engorged with the chicken that it had to climb over the fence instead of crawling underneath.

Police Chief Art Huey gathered up a crew of men of all ages who assembled outside the barbershop. It was a hunt of over 200 strong formed along Akron-Peninsula Road of reporters, sightseers, and locals armed with knives, ropes, pitchforks, and other hand-held weapons. They were also equipped with a whistle to blow should they come across the snake. Guns were banned, except for a single leader of each group who could be armed. The police chief advised the posse to take the animal alive. They hunted for part of the day, then came home empty-handed.

But the snake was still slithering around. The next Tuesday, Pauline Hopko living on Brandywine-Hudson Road, went to milk her dairy cows. They were nervous and agitated. She looked to a dead willow tree near the river and watched the head of a snake as big as a man's head slip out of the limbs.

On a quiet afternoon—Thursday, June 29th, Ernest Raymond, who lived on Brandywine-Twinsburg Road a couple of miles away from the Hopko's farm, was using a scythe to cut tall grass in an orchard on his own homestead. He looked up to see a gigantic snake coming out of the grass.

"I was leaning on the scythe and looking out this way," he relayed to an Akron Beacon Journal reporter. "I saw this thing and wondered who dragged that stump out here—hasn't been any stumps out here for a long time. Then I kept looking, and pretty soon, I see it starting to move from side to side. That head the size of a big kitchen pan came up out of the grass, and I could see the sun shining on the white part underneath." He headed to the house to get back-up from his son-in-law—and a shotgun. When the two returned, the snake was still there. However, a startled shout from one of the two frightened it away.

Kathryn Boroutich stood in horror when it dropped from a butternut tree near Peninsula and disappeared past the Cuyahoga River banks not far from the very first sighting. She darted toward home and fainted partway through her chicken yard. When she awakened, she called out an alarm, and a posse was formed. They never found the snake. Clifford Van Scoy, a farmer in West Jefferson, watched it rear its head back when he came upon it. Missus Ralph Griffith, Northfield Village, rounded up her six children with the speed of a mama bunny seeing a hawk flying overhead, and shuffled them to the safety of her house. "When I saw something that looked like a man in a white shirt about eighty feet away," she told reporters. "I blinked my eyes and saw it was a big snake. It was reared up shoulder high. His throat was white and shiny." It slithered off through the brush before she could seek out her neighbor with his shotgun.

Eight days later and seven miles away at Lee and Miles Road toward Cleveland, a couple of boys swimming in a rain-swollen creek saw the python. "We grabbed our clothes and ran up the hill," one of the frightened boys related to local police. "Then we put on our pants and ran home."

Just as quickly as it came causing a wild goose chase across the countryside, the snake slithered off into obscurity. No one has complained about the snake in a long time. Where it came from—many believed the python escaped from a circus trailer traveling through the Cuyahoga Valley—or where it went, no one is sure. Some say it died once winter set in. Others suggest it still could be living since industrial wastes tended to stop the river from freezing, and it just might harbor the snake in its warmer grasp.

The latter may be right. Over the years, a warm-weather snake was found dead along Eastlake Beach, and a non-native snake was killed in Rockbridge, Ohio, by a motorcyclist speeding down the highway. Could it possibly be breeding, you might ask? It might.

Where can you look for the Peninsula Python? You can follow the path of the elusive snake:

*Start along Akron Peninsula Road Near Everett Swamp—4192-3864 Akron Peninsula Road, Cuyahoga Falls, OH 44223 (41.194134, -81.566686)

Akron Peninsula Road near the Everett Swamps.

*Make a stop at the Everett Covered Bridge. There is a parking area where you can leave your car and hike 1.9 miles to the marsh:

Everett Covered Bridge Parking Lot: 2247 Everett Road, Peninsula, OH 44264 (41.204539, -81.580823)

Everett Covered Bridge.

*Hike to the Beaver Marsh Boardwalk View: 3801 Riverview Road (41.187933,-81.579450) Hop on the Valley Bridle Trail until it comes to the Ohio and Erie Towpath Trail. Hike to Beaver Marsh Boardwalk View (through the old swamps).

*After returning to your car, jump back on the road and head to Boston Store Visitor Center and the towpath trail – Ohio and Erie Canal Towpath vaguely follows the route the snake followed northward.

Boston Store—1550 Boston Mills Road. Peninsula, OH 44264 (41.263366, -81.558500)

Boston Store Visitor Center and the towpath trail.

*Lastly, head to the Brandywine Gorge Trail follows the Brandywine Creek where the farmer saw the snake.

8176 Brandywine Road Northfield, OH 44067

(41.277255, -81.538511)

Brandywine Falls Gorge.

Ohio

Camp Manatoc Red Eyes

Red Eye Madman of Camp Manatoc

Description: Headless apparition.

Other Names: Red Eyes. Ghost.

Location: Camp Manatoc Scout Reservation, Peninsula, Oh—Summit County

There is a legend told around the campfires of Camp Manatoc Scout Reservation in Cuyahoga National Park. It is about a camp ranger who died during the years of the Great Depression. Since he had no family to pay for a funeral, the camp decided to take it upon themselves to bury the man. They took up a collection, but no one had much money. As a result, the only coffin they could afford was child-size. And the ranger, he was a big, big man.

The camp administrators had a meeting. They had no clue how to solve the problem. One of them stood up and stated they did not have a choice—they would have to buy the small coffin, then chop the man into pieces to fit into the box. The rest agreed, they purchased the coffin, and they drew straws, and whoever drew the shortest straw would do the dirty deed. Such, one man drew that short straw, and he went about cutting and slicing, dicing, and sawing off the arms, legs, and head.

When the severed body was almost all packed, the head would not fit! Unbeknownst to anyone else at the time, the man nailed the coffin shut and buried the body parts in the coffin on the shore of Lake Litchfield. Then he took the head and buried it somewhere else, so nobody knew what he had done.

It was not long after that campers hiking in the woods at night began seeing two red dots in the darkness of the woods. When they shined their flashlights on it, they were horrified to see a floating head with no body—the man's head was looking for his body. And on some nights when dark clouds hid the moon, a camper would go out to collect firewood or visit the outhouse, and he never returned.

Where can you look for Camp Manatoc Red Eyes?

Camp Manatoc .

Camp Manatoc is a private Boy Scout Camp, but they do offer organization rentals.

1075 Truxell Road, Peninsula, OH 44264

(41.223558, -81.531029)

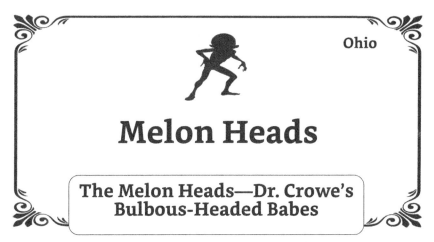

Ohio

Melon Heads

The Melon Heads—Dr. Crowe's Bulbous-Headed Babes

Description: Bulbous-heads. Humanoid.

Other Names: Melonheads.

Location: Kirtland, Oh—Lake County

Wisner Road, you can drive it. But don't go running into the woods. It is private property anywhere off the road proper.

You can hear them in the dark woods beside Wisner Road, their deep sorrowful moans, and their shrieking cries.

If you are lucky when you roll down your car window, you might hear the crunch of their tiny feet on broken branches and last year's autumn leaves before they see you. They are the Melon Heads of Kirtland, the tiny victims of a mad scientist's cruel experiments who run amok in what remains of the pockets of forest along Wisner Road that have not been taken over by private homes.

The dark passage of Wisner Road where the legend begins.

Dr. Crowe lived in a hidden pocket of woods near Kirtland, along Wisner Road in the 1950s. Within his care, he had orphans who suffered from hydrocephalus, a condition caused by excess fluid buildup in the brain. If left untreated, this condition hinders mental functioning, causes visual disorders, and makes it difficult to walk. He was supposed to be healing his small wards. Instead, he was conducting horrible scientific experiments on them. It left the children deformed with hairless heads and their minds, irrational. Many died during his procedures, but some lived. One night, they turned on the doctor and murdered him. Then, they ran into the woods, where they still live today.

Larned Cemetery.

Legends say that Doctor Crowe is buried in the Larned Cemetery in an unmarked grave with children he used for his sinister and twisted experiments. However, his young patients who broke free have long outlived their tormenter and have descendants wandering the woods. They are shy and appear as children with bulging, bulbous heads, roaming Wisner Road at night—eyes peering from the woods and screaming at those who cross their paths.

Where can you look for the Melon Heads?

The Melon Heads have always been connected to Wisner Road near Chardon. The mostly asphalt road weaves in and out of deep forest pockets and past farms and homes comes to a dead stop in some areas. The land on either side of the road is private. Another road paralleling it is Sperry Road and is near The Holden Arboretum—9550 Sperry Road, Kirtland, OH 44094. (41.608947, -81.299735) where there have been sightings along with a few at Larned Cemetery.

Ohio

South Bay Bessie

Lake Erie's Sea Monster

Description: Dark green or brown. Snake-like head. 30-40 feet long. Appears to undulate while it swims.

Other Names: Lake Erie Nessie.

Location: Throughout Lake Erie, notably around the shoreline near Sandusky and Cleveland, Oh

The Marblehead Lighthouse.

Lake Erie is shallow, warm, and the perfect environment for perch, walleye, and—the occasional monster. And there is a giant serpent-like creature lurking in the depths of Lake Erie. Its head has been bursting through the surface—and sometimes its entire body—for hundreds of years.

The first sighting recorded was from 1793 when the captain of the ship Felicity came across a sixteen-foot creature while hunting ducks near Sandusky, Ohio.

In May of 1897, it reared its head above the water near the Pelee Island Lighthouse high enough that the lightkeeper, William Grubb, got an eyeful. Adam Oper, a fisherman along the shore in his boat, was bringing in his nets when he looked up to see the water moving slightly before a huge head broke through. It was thirty feet long with a head that was disproportionately large and had horns and sharp teeth. A dorsal fin was raised above a scaled back, and the underparts went from white to red when it saw the fisherman. It made a long, loud hissing noise.

According to the Akron Beacon Journal in September of 1990, Dennis Szececinski of Toledo reported seeing the sea monster when fishing—described as long and black slithering in Maumee Bay near him Toledo's water intake structure. The same month, Harold Bricker, age 67, told Ohio State Park Rangers that he and his family were fishing north of Cedar Point Amusement Park. A thirty-foot serpent with a snake-like head swam by their boat.

In 1992, Charles Douglas—a fifty-five-year-old service station operator was heading out to fish for perch about ten miles off the shore of Vermilion on a fourth of July weekend when he saw something strange—he thought it was a big, dark log, but the thing was swimming. He throttled his boat up to about thirty miles per hour and, whatever it was, seemed to keep up with his pace. A couple of times, he increased the speed. He even steered toward the creature. Fearing he might hit something submerged in the water, he gave up and continued to his fishing spot.

This sea serpent has been described mainly as dark green or brown with a snake-like head, thirty to forty feet long, and appearing to undulate while it swims in the deep water.

In 1993, there had been a rash of sightings, including three boaters on two separate occasions. A captain of a fifty-two-foot charter boat saw a snake-like creature near Kellys Island. His wife saw it too. Unlike a snake, it moved its body, dipping up and down. It was fifteen to twenty feet long.

Most people call it the Lake Erie Monster, but a weekly newspaper in Port Clinton, Ohio, had a contest to name the serpent. The nickname South Bay Bessie won, and the name locally stuck. The creature tends to become quiet for decades at a time, resurfacing when least expected. From the large city of Toledo to the small town of Lakeside, you can pick a shoreline, snatch up a pair of binoculars and see if you can get a glimpse.

Where else can you look for South Bay Bessie?

*If you don't have a boat, you can try South Bay Bessie watching at these public accesses: **Bayview Park** on Summer Street in Toledo (41.695684, -83.477520) along with **Maumee Bay State Park** 1400 State Park Road, Oregon, OH 43616 (41.679801, -83.374157) and **Magee Marsh Wildlife Area** Park Road 1, Oak Harbor, OH 43449 (41.629334, -83.192913) are all within the region of the Toledo water intake structure—and maybe the serpent.*

Viewing Area: **Vermilion Lighthouse** *—480 Main Street Vermilion, OH 44089 (41.425057, -82.366575)*

Pipe Creek Wildlife Area (not far from Cedar Point sightings) F Street, Sandusky, OH 44870 (41.449696, -82.670010)

Take a ride to Kellys Island on the Kellys Island Ferry: *510 W Main St, Lakeside Marblehead, OH 43440*

Or take a ride to Put-In-Bay via Miller Boatline: *Miller Boat Line 5174 E Water Street Port Clinton, OH 43452*

A Monster from Pennsylvania

Monster/Cryptid	Map #
Lake Erie Storm Hag of Presque Isle	1

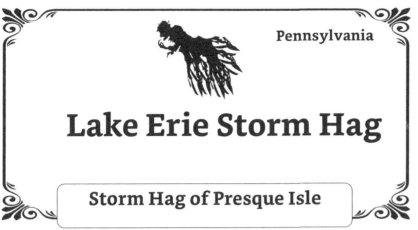

Pennsylvania

Lake Erie Storm Hag

Storm Hag of Presque Isle

Description: Ghastly pasty, green skin. Yellow eyes. Green teeth. Long fingers. Sharp fingernails.

Other Names: Demon Siren. Banshee. Jenny Greenteeth.

Location: Presque Isle Peninsula—Erie County, Pennsylvania

Presque Isle Bay is a peninsula arching into Lake Erie off the coast of Erie, Pennsylvania. Presque Isle State Park settled there offers swimming, boating, fishing, hiking, and more. You can drive the isle or walk the asphalt paths. Watch out toward the waters, mainly at Misery Bay for the wretched Storm Hag who has no pity for anyone sailing in her midst—

Presque Isle State Park
301 Peninsula Drive
Erie, PA 16505
(42.162733, -80.119675)

Presque Isle State Park is a sandy peninsula arching into Lake Erie near Erie, Pennsylvania. Lake Erie is prone to erratic waves, shifting sandbars, and wild, unpredictable storms. Its treacherous, shallow depths are known to harbor many shipwrecks up and down the coast—an estimated 500 to 3000 ships with their crews dragged down to a watery grave. Early explorers along the seventy-six miles of Pennsylvania's shorelines used this peninsula's eastern bay as a windbreak to beach boats during the many volatile storms. Not all those who sought its shelter made it out intact. The Lake Erie Quadrangle—a stretch of 2,500 square miles embracing an expansive shipwreck graveyard holds more wrecks than the Bermuda Triangle. Presque Isle is right amid its epicenter.

There is an ancient legend that explains the number of wrecks around Presque Isle. There is a Storm Hag who lives near the peninsula at the bottom of Lake Erie. She is ghastly with green, pasty skin, a pointed chin, and green locks of hair. Her arms are long and her nails sharp. Her eyes are yellow, and her green teeth are sharply pointed like a shark.

She emerges once in a while to feed upon those unfortunate sailors who come close to her lair. Before she attacks, she sings an enticing song that flows across the water. Then she calls up a ferocious storm to sink the boat and snatch up her meal. Sometimes she creeps to the land and hides in the trees waiting for little children to wander off from parents so she can stretch out her long arms and drag them to the water and drown them.

A storm settles into the horizon. Perhaps the Hag is within its midst, waiting for boaters to hurry to shore before she lets loose—

A traditional story of the Storm Hag's ruthlessness and Lake Erie's unpredictable squalls centers around a ship caught in a storm on Lake Erie in 1782. Seeing the black clouds rise on the horizon, the captain tried desperately to steer his ship toward Presque Isle's protective peninsula. To get to safety, he had to navigate past a dangerously shallow area before the storm hit, where many boats before him had gone down, trying with the same desperation to get to the shelter of the small bay. He did not make it and watched just short of the treacherous path while the waves beat his boat viciously side to side. He dared not take the risk.

As the sweat dribbled down his forehead and his men stared at him with frightened, knowing eyes, he felt the doom pass over him. In each man's gaze, he saw the grieving eyes of each mother and wife that he had let down by waiting too long. He would cause the ruin of his crew and the source of many a mourning mother and widowed wife. Suddenly, the storm stopped, and the clouds slipped away to moonlight shining off the calm waters. The sailors sighed, and the captain plotted a course through the shallows.

It was halfway through the dangerous shallows that they heard the soft song slipping through the breeze—the deep lulling wail a hearty wind makes passing through a nearly-closed window. *Come, lads, come. Tis safe, it is.* The men froze in horror as the moonlight dribbled away to darkness, and a foamy fog crept along with the clouds lurking across the sky. *The Siren. The Storm Hag.* She bestowed her fury on the ship in one bolt of lightning and a rousing smash of thunder. She burst from her lair in the bowels of the lake and attacked with the storm relentlessly until the boat vanished with its crew in the black depths.

Where can you find the Storm Hag?

Misery Bay view:
Thompson Drive
Erie, PA 16507
(42.160077, -80.086220)

Presque Isle Lighthouse
Presque Isle State Park,
301 Peninsula Drive, Millcreek
Township, PA 16505
(42.166055, -80.115398)

Those with a keen eye walking the shores of Presque Isle take note of tiny white crystals lying amidst the sand. It has been passed down that the crystals were made from the tears of the wives and mothers of sailors lured to their death by the Storm Hag after she let loose her fury and dragged the ship and crew into the dark waters below. When tucked into the palm, these crystals were used as charms to ward off the Hag and her wicked manipulation of the storms for her gain. Each unleashed a powerful rage from widows and mothers aimed at the Hag stealing the lives of loved ones.

Graveyard Pond Trail
Presque Isle State Park
Thompson Drive
(42.154724, -80.092714)

A traditional ghost story told on the isle reveals that in 1813, a fleet wintered at Little Bay on Presque Isle (Misery Bay) during a particularly unfriendly winter. While in the bay, the crew weathered it out on the boat or in makeshift tents on the shoreline. It was wet and frigid, and many took sick and died from Lake Fever (a common sailor label for any disease from malaria to typhoid fever). The corpses of those who died had to be disposed of quickly without last rites and a proper burial so that the living wrapped them in cloth and dumped them in Graveyard Pond. Unable to rest without appropriate rituals, their ghosts rise from the pond and walk toward the location the ship was moored.

A Monster from Kentucky

Monster/Cryptid	Map #
Goat-Man of Pope Lick Trestle	1

Kentucky

Goat-Man of Pope Lick Trestle

Pope Lick Monster

Description: Half-man, half-goat. Short, sharp horns. Protruding forehead. Fur-covered legs of a goat.

Other Names: Pope Lick Monster.

Location: Pope Lick—Jefferson County just outside Louisville, Ky

Built in the late 1800s, it rises 90 feet above Pope Lick, a tributary to Floyd's Fork in the Fisherville area of Louisville.

The trestle is 742 feet long, and Norfolk Southern trains still run across it. It has a hike/bike path running beneath it and a chain-link fence with warning signs: *Keep Off. Danger. Private Property.* And it has a grotesquely deformed half-goat, half-man that scares unwary visitors lurking beneath it. Yes, a Goat-Man with a penchant for killing people using voice mimicry or a siren-like call to lure them to their death.

The Pope Lick Monster balances on the girders beneath the trestle waiting for the unwary to pass along the road—or the bike trail.

Stories vary about how this creature came into existence—

—A nearby farmer whose land was wrought with drought and whose crops and livestock were dying made a pact with the devil by sacrificing goats, exchanging his soul for magical powers. As deals with the devils tend to go, the magical powers bestowed upon the farmer went awry, and the man was left as half-goat and half-demon to roam the area of his old farm.

—It is a half-goat hybrid, the offspring of a twisted farmer and his livestock.

—An evil circus ringmaster found a half-goat and half-child while traveling through Maryland. He treated the monster child with a cruel hand—forcing him to live in a cage and beating him to submission. When the train carrying the circus staff and tents crossed the trestle over Pope Lick, it derailed, killing almost everyone on board. The Goat-Boy escaped and ran into the woods.

The one thing the stories all have in common is that the Goat-Man lives on the girders and beneath the trestle. He lures people beneath the tracks and into the darkness with a low siren-like tone that hypnotizes his victims. He then lunges atop them where they vanish, never to return. Even looking at the beast in the eyes will cause people to go completely insane.

Over the years, many stories have distorted that of the legend—one involving crossing the trestle by foot. Trespassers have been struck by trains or fall off the bridge while climbing the trestle. In 2019, a 15-year-old girl died while clambering past the warning signs. The Goat-Man had not lured her there. In 2016, two Ohio tourists walking the rails and searching for the Goat-Man while in Louisville saw a train barreling their way with no time to run. Twenty-six-year-old Roquel Bain lost her life. The train was only moving thirty-two miles per hour. Nicholas Jewell, nineteen, died in 2000 trying to hold on to the side when he got caught by a train. In February 1988, Jack Bahm, a seventeen-year-old student from Spalding University, was struck and killed. In May of the previous year, nineteen-year-old David Bryant tried to jump and avoid a train after taking a dare to cross it. He died.

After researching the story, I could find absolutely no evidence the Goat-Man ever lured people *up to the trestle.*

Only recent urban legend trippers concocted the story of walking the tracks and manipulated the story so that Goat-Man lured the unwary to the railway above. In the original legends, Goat-Man always scampered *beneath* the tracks or *on the girders* waiting for passerby on horseback, carriage, car, or by foot. Then he would draw them into the darkness with a call or mimicking a familiar voice. Once in the shadows of the brush or woods, he would lunge and kill his quarry.

So, for those who climb the trestle or try to walk across the trestle, the only thing that will get them is a train. The genuine legendary Goat-Man of old is ninety-feet below those rails, down on the ground or slightly above up in the girders. If you want the thrill of actually contending with the beast, stick to the area underneath the trestle.

Where can you find the Goat-Man?

The legends tell that you must drive or walk underneath the trestle. Within the Parklands of Floyds Fork, the Louisville Loop (a 100-mile multi-recreational non-motorized path encircling the city) goes right under the Pope Lick Trestle before reaching Taylorsville Road. There is the Pope Lick Park Trailhead here. Hikers can walk over two miles, past John Floyd Fields and over the Pedestrian Bridge to the Big Beech Woods and Prairie Preserve. Stay off the trestle and railroad tracks; these are private property.

.

Citations:
Many of the monster renditions were made using monsters from TsuneoMP portfolio.
Snarly Yow:
-Dahlgren, M. V. (1882). South-Mountain Magic: A Narrative. McClain Printing Company.
-Map of Hiking Trails near Knoxville, Maryland | AllTrails. (n.d.). https://www.alltrails.com/explore/us/maryland/knoxville?a[] =hiking
-Map of the position at Turner's Gap. South Mountain. (n.d.). https://www.loc.gov/resource/gvhs01.vhs00120/? r=0.032,0.22,1.185,0.662,0
-A map of Washington Co., Maryland. Exhibiting the farms, election districts, towns, villages, roads, etc., etc. (n.d.). https:// www.loc.gov/item/2002624033/
Snallygaster:
-Will Questions About Bigfoot-Things Ever Stop? Frederick News Post Leader November 2, 1988
-Add Snallygaster. 9/7/1951 The Evening Sun [Maryland], p. 30.
-Beasties Rode at Night? Monsters Sought at Sykesville. (1973, June 10). Frederick News Post[Frederick Md],
-Boyton, P. (2011). Snallygaster: The Lost Legend of Frederick County. Morrisville, NC: Lulu.com.
-Burns, J. R. (2008, October 28). The Snallygaster. appalachianlifestyles. blogspot.com /2008/10/snallygaster.html
-M Ernesto Bughooey Visits the Quirauk Wilds. (1908, January 10). Hagerstown Mail.
-SNALLYGASTER ON THE LOOSE IN SYKESVILLE. (1973, June 13). The Capital[Annapolis, MD], p. 9.
-Snallygaster – Winged Creature of the Northeast – Legends of America. (n.d.). https://www.legendsofamerica.com/ snallygaster/ (The —Pendleton Times, Franklin, WV. March 1, 1935; May 10, 1935; February 14, 1941; July 11, 1941; and April 5 & 12, 1946.)
-"True says one faction," Says one faction, "Nothing to it . ... (1932, November 28). The_News_Mon [Frederick (Maryland)].
-Flying saucers pretty tame beside flying snallygaster. (1947, Jul 08). The Sun (1837-1993) search-proquest-com.research.cincinnatilibrary.org/docview/542697404? accountid=39387
Dwayyo:
-Dwayyo – The Maryland Wolf Man – Legends of America. (n.d.). https://www.legendsofamerica.com/dwayyo/
-ELUSIVE DWAYYO STILL UNCAPTURED. (1965, December 2). The News. May, George. Staff Writer. (1865, December 1). DWAYYO -—MONSTER IS STILL RUNNING LOOSE. The News [Frederick, Md].
-MYSTERIOUS "DWAYYO" ON LOOSE IN COUNTY. (1965, November 29). THE NEWS[FREDERICK].
-Steiger, B. (2011). The Dwayyo. In The Werewolf Book: The Encyclopedia of Shape-Shifting Beings. Visible Ink Press.
-Haunted Hikes: Phantoms Of The Northern Appalachian Trails .... https://historycollection.co/haunted-hikes-phantoms-of-the-northern-appalachian-trails-are-the-remainders-of-a-bloody-civil-war-battle/
Sykesville Monster:
-BFRO Report 231: Man witness confrontation between bigfoot and stray dog, near Sykesville. https://www.bfro.net/GDB/ show_report.asp?id=231
-'Sykesville Monster' Encounter. (n.d.). https://-www.phantomsandmonsters.com/p/the-sykesville-encounter.html

Goatman (Maryland):
-Frizzell, Michael. (n.d.). A Synopsis of the History, Reports, and Investigation of Claims of Unknown Hominids in and about the State of Maryland. http://www.enigmaproject.org/
-Goldman, Ivan G. (1971, December 10). Goatman: Is He Real or Phantom? Los Angeles Times.
-Hosler, Karen. (1971, November 10). Residents Fear Goatman Lives: Dog Found Decapitated in Old Bowie. Prince George's County News.
-A Legendary Figure Haunts Remote Pr. George's Woods: Edge of the Wood. (1971, November 30). The Washington Post, Times Herald.
-MCHUGH, JANE. (2007, October 19). Goatman legend lives on in Bowie.

Chessie:
-Bay Monster. (1982, July 12). The Washington Post
- BAY MONSTER - The Washington Post. https://www.washingtonpost.com/archive/local/1982/07/12/bay-monster/ef74e6be-4b4f-45dc-8933-7bc72b3e98ed/
-May, A. (2017, October 31). Legend of Chessie alive, well in Maryland. https://www.wbaltv.com/article/legend-of-chessie-alive-well-in-maryland/13126354
-(1876, August 16). New Orleans Republican.
-Report Sea Serpent in Chesapeake Bay. (1934, June 7). The New Journal.
-TWO SEA SERPENTS IN THE CHESAPEAKE BAY. (1846, February 27). American Republican and Baltimore Daily Clipper [Baltimore, MC], p. 1.

Flatwoods Monster:
-Flatwoods Monster Museum Andrew Smith, Executive Director Braxton County Visitor Bureau
-Flatwoods Monster. (n.d.). Http://www.braxtonwv.org/FlatwoodsMonsterInfo.aspxFeschino, F. C. (2012). The Braxton County Monster: The Cover-up of the "Flatwoods Monster" Revealed.
-Flatwoods Monster http://www.flatwoodsmonster.com/ Wenzl, R. (2018, 20). In 1952, the Flatwoods Monster Terrified 6 Kids, a Mom, a Dog and the Nation.
-BRAXTON COUNTY WOMAN FEELS GLOWING OBJECT WAS JET SHIP. (1956, October 6). Charleston Gazette.
-Flatwoods Phantom Gave Braxton Folks Something to Talk About Two Years Ago. (1954, September 11). Charleston Daily Mail [Charleston].
-Martian or Mirage. (1954, October 30). Charleston Gazette [Charleston].
-MONSTER SITE REVISITED. (1959, September 15). Charleston Daily Mail.
-SEE MONSTER. (1952, September 17). Creston News Advertizer [Creston, Iowa].

Hellhounds:
-Keith Hammersla, Director of Information Services at Martinsburg Public Library and resident genealogist
-"Percolated" (weekly column). (Ghost Seen on Church Street). Martinsburg
News, March 14, 1947, pages 1 and 8.
-"Know Your Martinsburg" (weekly column) by F.B. Voegele. (Ghosts in
Cemeteries). Martinsburg News, April 4, 1947, page 1.
-"Comments on County History" by F.B. Voegele, (Ghost Dogs of East Burke Street). Martinsburg News, August 25, 1939, pages 1 and 8.

Tommyknockers:
-Cooper's Clarksburg register., January 19, 1853.
-Bluefield Daily Telegraph—Tommyknockers the Miners' Ghost

Mothman:
-Eight People Say The Saw 'Creature. (1966, November 17). The Raleigh Register.
-Flying Man' Seen Here, Man Claims. (11/18/1966). Charleston Gazette.
-FLYING "WHATEVER IT WAS" A RED-EYED MYSTERY. (1966, November 18). The Tennessean [NASHVILLE], p. 47.
-Grave. (n.d.). www.findagrave.com/memorial/100081454/homer-smith Kenneth Duncan's Mothman Sighting. (n.d.). https://themothman.fandom.com/wiki/Kenneth_Duncan%27s_Mothman_Sighting
-MISSING SHEPHERD DOG ADDED TO PREY OF CREATURE. (1966, November 18). The Daily Notes [Canonsburg, Pennsylvania], p. 10.
-The Mothman of Point Pleasant - 13 Months That Changed History [Television series episode]. (1017, June 2). In Seth Breedlove (Producer), "Small Town Monsters".
-The Mothman Timeline. themothman.fandom.com/wiki/The_Mothman_Timeline
The Original Mothman Police Reports Available to be seen at Mothman Museum in Point Pleasant owner, Jeff Wamsley. (n.d.).
-Original Mothman Police Reports. themothman.fandom.com/wiki/—The_Original_Mothman_Police_Reports
Sergent, D., & Wamsley, J. (2002). Mothman: The Facts Behind the Legend. Mothman Lives Publishing.
-Did legendary Mothman first appear at Clendenin cemetery …. https://wvexplorer.com/2019/06/01/did-legendary-mothman-first-appear-at-clendenin-cemetery/
Sheepsquatch:
-Exploring American Monsters: West Virginia. (2016, July 29). mysteriousuniverse.org/2017/03/exploring-american-monsters-west-virginia/
-Sheepsquatch (Breckenridge County, KY) [Television series episode]. (2013, March 24). In Monsters and Mysteries in America. Destination America.
-Sheepsquatch: A creature from the past. (n.d.). https://yeahstub.com/sheepsquatch-a-creature-from-the-past/
Flying Rays:
-Flying Manta Rays. (n.d.). themothman.fandom.com/wiki/Flying_Manta_Rays
-https://cryptidchronicles.tumblr.com/post/38161391663/winged-manta-ray-shaped-cryptid-near-ashton-west-virginia
-Prather, Terry. (2014, September 19). Ledger Independent. Maysville, KY Dead shark found along Manchester shore. maysville-online.com/news/local/dead-shark-found-along-manchester-shore/
-https://ufo.blogflop.com/2018/10/14/cryptidchronicleswinged-manta-ray-shaped-cry/
Wampus Cat:
-Have You Ever Heard of Appalachia's Wampus Cat Legend? (2017, March 31). appalachianmagazine.com/2017/03/31/have-you-ever-heard-of-appalachias-wampus-cat-legend/
-http://www.wvdnr.gov/wildlife/magazine/-Archive/05Fall/coldknob.pdf. (n.d.). http://www.wvdnr.gov/wildlife/magazine/Archive/05Fall/coldknob.pdf
-A JUNGLE OUT THERE? A HUNTER SAYS LION IN WOODS. (2007, October 24). Beckley Register Herald.
-Samples, M. (2005). The Wampus Cat at King Shoals. In The Devil's Tea Tables: West Virginia Ghost Stories and Other Tales.
-The Wampus Cat. (n.d.). northcarolinaghosts.com/mountains/wampus-cat/

White Thing:
-Fairmont to 459 Morgan Ridge Rd. (n.d.). https://
www.google.com/maps/dir/
Fairmont,+WV+26554/459+Morgan+Ridge+Rd,+Rivesville,+WV
/@39.5450718,-80.0978125,124m/data=!3m1!1e3!4m14!4m13!
1m5!1m1!1s0x884a7ddaaa5f7171:0xda7771214d47916b!2m2!
1d-80.1425781!2d39.4850848!1m5!1m1!
1s0x884a8009e6e239d5:0x9e83cf7c5f783607!2m2!1d-
80.097724!2d39.544145!3e0
-Musick, R. A. (2010). Chapter 92 White Thing Chapter 93 -The
Strange Creature. In The Telltale Lilac Bush and Other West
Virginia Ghost Tales. Lexington, KY: University Press of ky
-White Things (Devil Dogs). (n.d.). https://cryptidz.fandom.com/
wiki/White_Things_(Devil_Dogs)
WV Coal Mining. (n.d.). http://www.wvgs.wvnet.edu/GIS/CBMP/
all_mining.html
Grafton Monster:
-Apples Devils and The Grafton Monster. (n.d.).
themothman.fandom.com/wiki/
Apples_Devils_and_The_Grafton_Monster
-The Grafton Monster, Grafton West Virginia | Unsolved
Mysteries of the World. (n.d.). https://shows.pippa.io/unsolved-
mysteries-of-the-world/episodes/the-grafton-monster-grafton-
west-virginia
-Fallout76 - Braxton CVB. http://www.braxtonwv.org/
fallout76.aspx
Cumberland Dragon:
-Cumberland Dragon. (n.d.). https://cryptidz.fandom.com/wiki/
Cumberland_Dragon
-Curious Animal. (1794, September 13). Pittsburgh Evening
Gazette [Pittsburgh].
-(1794, September 30). The_Farmers Library of Vermont Political
Historical Register.
-Forum | Cryptozoology & Monsters | Egertron Puck's Modern
Bestiary. (n.d.). knegerton.wixsite.com/mysite/forum-1/
creature-discussion/tentative-list-of-wv-creatures-to-be-added
-Monsters in the Southwest Territory. (2017, February 11).
boston1775.blogspot.com/2017/02/monsters-in-southwest-
territory.html
Marrtown Banshee:
KILLED. THOMAS MARR. (1874, February 17). Parkersburg
Examiner [PARKERSBURG].
Giant Birds:
-EAGLE TRIED TO CARRY BOY AWAY. (1907, May 14). The
Fairmont West_Virginian[FAIRMONT], p. 5.
-GIGANTIC BIRD OF THE GAULEY RIVER MOUNTAINEERS
TERRORIZED BY A FEATHERED MONSTER TEN YEAR OLD
CHILD CARRIED AWAY. (1895, March 2). The Cincinnati
Enquirer [Cincinnati], p. 12.
-A MODERN ROC. (1895, March 16). Evening Star, p. 18.
Newton, M. (2015). Roc Around the Clock.
-O'dell, Les. Bigfoot footprint on mountain.
Wendigo:
-A WEIRD STORY OF A GHOSTLY NOISE. (1928, June 9). The
Ottawa Citizen.
-Wendigo – Flesheater of the Forests – Legends of America. (n.d.).
https://www.legendsofamerica.com/mn-wendigo/
Vegetable Man:
-https://cryptidz.fandom.com/wiki/Veggieman
-Michaels, Denver Wild & Wonderful (and Paranormal) West
Virginia

Bigfoot:
-High definition scan of the iconic "Frame 352" - Ep 139: The Patterson-Gimlin Film Part 1. (2019, April 14). https://www.astonishinglegends.com/al-podcasts/2019/4/13/ep-139-the-patterson-gimlin-film-part-1
-Barackman, C. (2013, April 20). 2007 West Virginia Footprint. http://www.northamericanbigfoot.com/2013/04/2007-west-virginia-footprint.html
-Angel marks the trail at Salt Fork's Hosak's Cave in Ohio. (2016, May 2). https://www.denverpost.com/2011/09/14/angel-marks-the-trail-at-salt-forks-hosaks-cave-in-ohio/
-BFRO Report 25301: Hunter has close sighting of a primate-like creature in the Canaan Valley National Wildlife Refuge - Bigfoot Field Researchers Organization (BFRO). (n.d.). http://www.bfro.net/GDB/show_report.asp?id=25301
-BFRO Report 3920: Hunters have several encounters near Ash Cave State Park. (n.d.). http://www.bfro.net/GDB/show_report.asp?id=3920
-Bigfoot at Salt Fork? (n.d.). http://www.mabrc.com/forums/backupweb/eobic/082004jeff.html
-Giggenbach, C. (2014, July 29). More than 50 Bigfoot sightings tallied in W.Va. https://www.register-herald.com/news/local_news/more-than-bigfoot-sightings-tallied-in-w-va/article_9043d0d8-44f6-56cd-aa9e-77cfda7c2d47.html
-Home - Braxton CVB. (n.d.). http://www.braxtonwv.org/
-Jones, Russell Dr., R. (2016). Tracking the Stone Man: West Virginia's Bigfoot.
-Motorist sees hairy biped crossing road by Cuyahoga Valley National Park. (n.d.). http://squatchable.com/report.asp?id=2902&title=Motorist+sees+hairy+biped+crossing+road+by+Cuyahoga+Valley+National+Park
-O'Dell, L. (n.d.). WV Cryptids and Strange Encounters. https://www.facebook.com/wvcryptidsandstrangeencounters/photos/a.736803089864045/829641060580247?type=3&sfns=mo
-O'Dell, Les. (n.d.). WV Cryptids and Strange Encounters. https://www.facebook.com/wvcryptidsandstrangeencounters
-Recent bigfoot sightings at Sutton Lake have historic precedent. (2019, February 1). https://wvexplorer.com/2019/01/30/bigfoot-sightings-at-sutton-lake-have-historic-precedent/
-RETURN OF WILDMAN REVIVES OLD TERRORS. (1919, March 8). The Evening Telegram [Lakeland, Florida].
-Richwood to Camden-On-Gauley. (n.d.). -https://goo.gl/maps/nCJwmu3CoQTgCcg6A
-Steelhammer, R. (2017, November 21). Dunbar chiropractor writes the book on West Virginia Bigfoot lore. https://www.wvgazettemail.com/_arts__entertainment/dunbar-chiropractor-writes-the-book-on-west-virginia-bigfoot-lore/article_9bdc3ef0-255d-54fb-a908-31350f379d8c.html
-WV Cryptids and Strange Encounters. (n.d.). https://www.facebook.com/wvcryptidsandstrangeencounters/photos/a.736803089864045/829641060580247?type=3&sfns=mo
-Braxton Monster Real Thing, Kanawha Man's Letter Reveals. (1961, January 4). CHARLESTON DAILY MAIL [CHARLESTON],
-BRAXTON MONSTER REPORTEDLY SEEN BY TRUCKER. (1961, January 1). Beckley Post Herald Register [BECKLEY], pp. p-5.
-IS BRAXTON MONSTER BACK? TRUCKER BELIEVES SO. (1960, December 30). Charleston Daily-Mail [Charleston], pp. 1, 3.
-(1978, August 16). The Independent Herald [Pineville].
WV Cryptids and Strange Encounters. (n.d.). -https://www.facebook.com/wvcryptidsandstrangeencounters/photos/

a.736803089864045/822936177917402/?type=3&theater
https://www.bfro.net/GDB/show_county_reports.asp?
state=wv&county=Pendleton
-BFRO Media Article 111. http://bfro.net/GDB/show_article.asp?
id=111
-The Columbia River - Sasquatch (Bigfoot). http://
columbiariverimages.com/Regions/Places/sasquatch.html
-Washington State Counties – Page 6 – Washington Bigfoot.
https://washingtonbigfoot.com/category/county/page/6/
-Blackwater Falls State Park, a West Virginia State Park ....
https://www.stateparks.com/blackwater_falls.html
-Apples Devils and The Grafton Monster | TheMothMan Wikia ....
https://themothman.fandom.com/wiki/
Apples_Devils_and_The_Grafton_Monster
-BFRO Report 34043: Observation by a hunter through his ....
http://www.bfro.net/GDB/show_report.asp?id=34043
-Dunbar chiropractor writes the book on West Virginia ....
https://www.wvgazettemail.com/_arts__entertainment/dunbar
-chiropractor-writes-the-book-on-west-virginia-bigfoot-lore/
article_9bdc3ef0-255d-54fb-a908-31350f379d8c.html
-Dudding, G. (n.d.). The Oceana Monster.

Ogua:
-https://depositphotos.com/stock-photos/cherokee-at-campfire-
st60.html?filter=all
-https://depositphotos.com/stock-photos/native-indian-furs-
st60.html?filter=all&qview=4455286

Minerva Monster:
-Creature Hunters Invade Stark. (1978, August 27). Akron Beacon
Journal [Akron].
-"Creatures" Stalk Rural Stark Home. (1978, August 23). Akron
Beacon Journal [Akron].
-Mudrak, B. (1978, August 24). CRICKETS QUIET WHEN THE
"CREATURE" PROWLS. The Akron Beacon Journal [AKRON].
-Mudrak, Barbara. (1980, June 29). Minerva's Monster is almost a
Pet. Akron Beacon Journal[Akron].
-What was it? Man talks about 'Minerva Monster' mystery 40
years later. (2017, October 31). https://fox8.com/2017/10/31/
what-was-it-man-talks-about-minerva-monster-mystery-40-
years-later/

Loveland Frogman:
-17 Oct 1973, Page 1 - The Cincinnati Enquirer at
Newspapers.com. (n.d.). https://www.newspapers.com/
image/104466541/?terms=loveland%2B1955%2Bfrog
-Budd, D. W. (2010). The Weiser Field Guide to Cryptozoology:
Werewolves, Dragons, Skyfish, Lizard Men, and Other
Fascinating Creatures Real and Mysterious. Weiser Books.
-Davis, I., & Bloecher, T. (1978). Hunnicutt's Strange Story.
In Close Encounter at Kelly and Others of 1955.
-Davis, I., & Bloecher, T. (1978). THE LOVELAND BRIDGE CASE.
In Close Encounter at Kelly and Others of 1955.
-Davis, ISABEL. (1978). CLOSE ENCOUNTER AT KELLY AND
OTHERS OF 1955(Unpublished doctoral dissertation). CENTER
FOR UFO STUDIES.
-Davis, Isabel. (n.d.). Chapter VI The Loveland Bridge Case.
In Close Encounter at Kelly.
-Frozen iguanas falling from trees during cold snap in Florida.
(2018, January 4). https://www.cbsnews.com/news/florida-
frozen-iguanas-falling-from-trees-during-cold-snap-bomb-
cyclone-storm-east-coast/
-Hedeen, Stanley. (n.d.). History of the Little Miami River - Little

Miami Conservancy. Little Miami Conservancy website: http://littlemiami.com/LITTLE%20MIAMI%20RIVER%20ECOLOGY%20AND%20HISTORY.pdf

-Legend of the Humanoid Loveland Frog Comes to Local Stage at Fringe Fest. (2014, May 27). https://www.rcnky.com/articles/2014/05/27/legend-humanoid-loveland-frog-comes-local-stage-fringe-fest

-Loveland - Showing the Different Subdivision Including The Heights. (n.d.). https://www.google.com/maps/place/Loveland,+OH/@39.2635155,-84.2877482,14z/data=!4m5!3m4!1s0x884055fca1f6dc2b:0x70ddec8d2276862c!8m2!3d39.2689476!4d-84.263826

-The Loveland Frogmen. (2017, November 9). https://www.singularfortean.com/singularjournal/2017/11/8/the-loveland-frogmen

-Officer reveals true story of Loveland Frogman. (2016, August 6). https://www.wcpo.com/news/local-news/hamilton-county/loveland-community/officer-who-shot-loveland-frogman-in-1972-says-story-is-a-hoax

-Page 72 Project Blue Book - UFO Investigations. (n.d.). https://www.fold3.com/image/7073676

-Renner, J. (2012). It Came from Ohio: True Tales of the Weird, Wild, and Unexplained. Gray & Company, Publishers.

-Scott, J. (2016, August 19). Local legend: Does the Loveland Frogman live on? http://www.fox19.com/story/32688947/legend-of-loveland-frogman-lives-on/

-U.S. Weather History Back to 1945 from the Farmers' Almanac. (n.d.). https://www.farmersalmanac.com/weather-history/search-results/

Ohio River Sea Serpent:

-11 Jan 1878, Page 4 - The Cincinnati Enquirer at - Newspapers.com. (n.d.). https://www.newspapers.com/image/31289606/?terms=%22river%2Bmonster%22

(1880, February 8). CINCINNATI GAZETTE.

-Sea Serpents in the Ohio River (And Other Cincinnati Monsters). (2016, November 1). https://www.cincinnatimagazine.com/citywiseblog/sea-serpents-ohio-river-cincinnati-monsters/

Crosswick Monster:

-Dixon, Roy. (1978, June 11). MONSTERS in Your Own Backyard. The Dayton Daily News[Dayton].

-SNAIX. (1882, May 29). The Cincinnati Enquirer.

Cedar Bog Monster:

-Weird Ohio. (n.d.). http://www.weirdus.com/states/ohio/bizarre_beasts/bigfoot_cedar_bog/index.php

Devil Monkey:

-Devil. (1875, March 25). Gallipolis Journal.

-Eberhart, G. M. (2002). Mysterious Creatures: A Guide to Cryptozoology. Santa Barbara, CA: ABC-CLIO.

-The Mysterious Devil Monkeys of North America. (2017, February 22). https://mysteriousuniverse.org/2018/06/the-mysterious-devil-monkeys-of-north-america/

-Virginia's Mysterious Devil Monkey Sightings | Appalachian http://appalachianmagazine.com/2017/04/27/virginias-mysterious-devil-monkey-sightings/

Delphos Dogman and Defiance Wolfman:

-Defiance Residents Suspicious of their Werewolf. (1972, August 4). Toledo Blade [Toledo].

-"The Werewolf of Defiance" is an Ohio local legend that still haunts. (2019, January 30). http://www.cleweekend.com/werewolf-defiance-ohio-local-legend-still-haunts-town/

-WEREWOLF CASE IN DEFIANCE NOT VIEWED LIGHTLY BY POLICE. (1972, August 3). Toledo Blade [TOLEDO].
The Werewolf Page Myths - Werewolf of Defiance. (n.d.). http://werewolfpage.com/myths/Defiance%20.htm
-WEREWOLF REPORTED IN SENECA. (1972, August 4). Findlay Republican Courier.
-The Black Swamp Journal | History of the Great Black Swamp. (2011, April 14). https://blogs.bgsu.edu/blackswampjournal/2011/04/14/history-of-the-great-black-swamp/
-Cryptids, C. (2006, November 1). American Werewolf or Sasquatch? https://cryptomundo.com/bigfoot-report/werewolf/
Dane, C. (1973). The American Indian and the Occult.
-Resurrection Cemetery and Werewolf. (n.d.). Delphos Herald [Delphos].
-The Werewolf Page Myths - Werewolf of Defiance. http://werewolfpage.com/myths/Defiance%20.htm

Charles Lake Monsters:
-Boys Report Seeing Green Eyed Monster News-Journal at Newspapers.com. (1959, March 28).
-Orange Eyes and the Charles Mill Lake Monster. (n.d.). https://www.phantomsandmonsters.com/2012/09/orange-eyes-and-charles-mill-lake.html
-Day, Courtney. (n.d.). Investigators seek UFO witnesses. Mansfield News Journal.
-ORANGE EYES: (OHIO, USA). (2012, November 25). https://www.cryptopia.us/site/2010/01/orange-eyes-ohio-usa/

Peninsula Python:
-TRUCK OVERTURNS, CIRCUS MAN DIES. (1942, June 18). The Akron Beacon Journal[Akron].
-13 Jul 1944, Page 1 - The Akron Beacon Journal at Newspapers.com. (n.d.). https://www.newspapers.com/image/146538707/?terms=peninsula%2Bpython
-15 Feb 1959, Page 85 - The Akron Beacon Journal at Newspapers.com. (n.d.). https://www.newspapers.com/image/148467883/?terms=peninsula%2Bpython%2Bbrandywine
-2 Jul 1944, Page 2 - The Akron Beacon Journal at Newspapers.com. (n.d.). https://www.newspapers.com/image/146537849/?terms=peninsula%2Bpython%2BPauline%2BHopko
-30 Jun 1944, Page 1 - The Akron Beacon Journal at Newspapers.com. (n.d.). https://www.newspapers.com/image/146537686/
-5 Jul 1944, Page 1 - Delphos Daily Herald at Newspapers.com. (n.d.). https://www.newspapers.com/image/15176957/?terms=peninsula%2Bpython
-The Journal Herald at Newspapers.com Peninsula Python Still at Large. (1944, June 26).
Mitten, R. (1944, June 26). Peninsula Python Searchers Find - How Sore Unused Muscles. The Akron Beacon Journal.
-Snakes on a Flood Plain: Python Hysteria in Ohio. (2012, July 5). http://weekinweird.com/2012/07/05/snakes-flood-plain-python-hysteria-ohio/
-What Was the Fate of Peninsula Python. (1959, February 15). The Akron Beacon Journal.

Camp Manatoc:
-Red Eyes, the Mad Man of Camp Manatoc. (n.d.). http://tylerscryptozoo.blogspot.com/2018/05/red-eyes-mad-man-of-camp-manatoc.html

Melon Heads:
Melonheads of Kirtland/Chardon? (n.d.). http://
northcoastview.blogspot.com/2009/10/melonheads-of-
kirtlandchardon.html
Urban legend or truth? Tale of the Melon Heads in Kirtland.
(2014, October 31). https://fox8.com/2014/10/31/urban-legend
-or-truth-tale-of-the-melon-heads-in-kirtland/
South Bay Bessie:
21 Sep 1990, Page 15 - The Akron Beacon Journal at
Newspapers.com. (n.d.). https://www.newspapers.com/
image/156697653/
HISSING. HEAD REARED ABOVE WAVES. (1897, May 29). The
Cincinnati Enquirer at Newspapers.com, p. 1.
Lake Erie monster tales resurface. (1993, July 19). The News-
Messenger [Fremont].
LAKE ERIE MONSTER. (1993, October 28). Calgary Herald at
Newspapers.com.
Sea Serpents in the Ohio River (And Other Cincinnati Monsters).
(2016, November 1). https://www.cincinnatimagazine.com/
citywiseblog/sea-serpents-ohio-river-cincinnati-monsters/
Presque Isle Storm Hag:
-10 Creepy Urban Legends From Pennsylvania Not For The Faint Of Heart.
(2015, April 1). https://www.onlyinyourstate.com/pennsylvania/pa-
urbanlegends/
-http://www.examiner.com/examiner/x-4872-Pittsburgh-Paranormal-
Examiner~y2009m4d17-The-Lake-Erie-Storm-Hag-demonic-siren-of-
the-Great-Lakes
-Hunting for shipwrecks in Presque Isle's Misery Bay. (2018, March 8). —
-http://www.rockthelake.com/buzz/2018/02/hunting-for-shipwrecks-
in-presque-isles-misery-bay/
-Jenny Green Teeth : Internet Archive. (n.d.). https://archive.org/details/
donald_002
-The Lake Erie 'Storm Hag', demonic siren of the Great Lakes. (n.d.).
http://theparanormalpastor.blogspot.com/2009/04/lake-erie-storm-hag
-demonic-siren-of.html
Goat-Man: Pope Lick Trestle-Kentucky
-ALONG THE NEW ROUTE: Description of the Course Taken By the
Louisville Southern Passing Through a Country of Picturesque Beauty On
the Way To Harrodsburg Fisherville and Jeffersontown . . .. (1888, April
30). Louisville Courier Journal[Louisville].
-Pope Lick Monster. (n.d.). https://www.facebook.com/PopeLickMonster/
-Tourist dies on search for Pope Lick monster. (2016, April 24). https://
www.courier-journal.com/story/news/local/2016/04/24/tourist-dies-
search-pope-lick-monster/83470646/
-The Courier-Journal Louisville, Kentucky 19 Feb 1988, Fri · Page 8
-Louisville Loop | The Parklands of Floyds Fork. https://
www.theparklands.org/Parks/The-Strand/10/Louisville-Loop